The *Resetting Our F* [barcode: T0041427]

At this critical moment of history, with a pandemic raging, we have the rare opportunity for a Great Reset – to choose a different future. This series provides a platform for pragmatic thought leaders to share their vision for change based on their deep expertise. For communities and nations struggling to cope with the crisis, these books will provide a burst of hope and energy to help us take the first difficult steps towards a better future.
– Tim Ward, publisher, Changemakers Books

What if Solving the Climate Crisis Is Simple?
Tom Bowman, President of Bowman Change, Inc., and writing-team lead for the U.S. ACE National Strategic Planning Framework

Zero Waste Living, the 80/20 Way
The Busy Person's Guide to a Lighter Footprint
Stephanie Miller, Founder of Zero Waste in DC, and former Director, IFC Climate Business Department

A Chicken Can't Lay a Duck Egg
How COVID-19 Can Solve the Climate Crisis
Graeme Maxton (former Secretary-General of the Club of Rome) and Bernice Maxton-Lee (former Director, Jane Goodall Institute)

A Global Playbook for the Next Pandemic
Anne Kabagambe, former World Bank Executive Director

Power Switch
How We Can Reverse Extreme Inequality
Paul O'Brien, Executive Director, Amnesty International USA

Impact ED
How Community College Entrepreneurship Creates Equity and Prosperity
Rebecca Corbin (President & CEO, National Association of Community College Entrepreneurship), Andrew Gold and Mary Beth Kerly (both business faculty, Hillsborough Community College)

Empowering Climate Action in the United States
Tom Bowman (President of Bowman Change, Inc.) and Deb Morrison (Learning Scientist, University of Washington)

Learning from Tomorrow
Using Strategic Foresight to Prepare for the Next Big Disruption
Bart Édes, former North American Representative, Asian Development Bank

Cut Super Climate Pollutants, Now!
The Ozone Treaty's Urgent Lessons for Speeding Up Climate Action
Alan Miller (former World Bank representative for global climate negotiations), Durwood Zaelke (President and founder, the Institute for Governance & Sustainable Development) and Stephen O. Andersen (former Director of Strategic Climate Projects at the Environmental Protection Agency)

Resetting Our Future: Long Haul COVID: A Survivor's Guide
Transform Your Pain & Find Your Way Forward
Dr. Joseph J. Trunzo (Professor of Psychology and Department Chair at Bryant University) and Julie Luongo (author of *The Hard Way*)

SMART Futures for a Flourishing World
A Paradigm Shift for Achieving Global Sustainability
Dr. Claire Nelson, Chief Visionary Officer and Lead Futurist,
The Futures Forum

Rebalance
How Women Lead, Parent, Partner and Thrive
Monica Brand, Lisa Neuberger & Wendy Teleki

Provocateurs not Philanthropists:
Turning Good Intentions into Global Impact
Maiden R. Manzanal-Frank, President and CEO, GlobalStakes
Consulting, and Instructor-Coach, Rotary Center for
International Studies in Peace, Conflict Transformation, and
Development, Chulalongkorn University

Resetting the Table
Nicole Civita (Vice President of Strategic Initiatives at Sterling
College, Ethics Transformation in Food Systems) and Michelle
Auerbach

Unquenchable Thirst
How Water Rules the World and How Humans Rule Water
Luke Wilson and Alexandra Campbell-Ferrari (Co-Founders of
the Center for Water Security and Cooperation)

www.ResettingOurFuture.com

What people are saying about

Resetting Our Future
Provocateurs not Philanthropists

We all want to make an impact on the world—to leave it better than we found it—but this can feel overwhelming and confusing. Maiden Manzanal-Frank has written the ultimate guide to understanding impact, backed with research and firsthand experience, and practical steps to start giving back today. No matter where you are in your life or career, this book will change your life!

Dr. Marshall Goldsmith, Thinkers50 #1 Executive Coach and *New York Times* bestselling author of *Triggers, Mojo*, and *What Got You Here Won't Get You There*

"We need system change" is often heard when talking about solutions for the many crises the world is going through. For that, we need leaders who urge for radical change, out-of-the-box, and building new systems on all levels. You could call them "provocateurs," the ones that provoke change towards a sustainable, fair, and humane society. We have many of those provocateurs already, but we need more! This easy-reading book will wake up the audience and let them realize how to become an impact leader towards the urgently needed system change.

Leida Rijnhout, Chief Executive, World Fair Trade Organization (WFTO)

The world is full of people who mean well and have good intentions to solve global issues, but many wonder how? Here is a book that focuses on "impact" versus tick-in-the-box good works. Now you can have a measurable impact on all you want to do.

Dr. Ravi A. Fernando, Chairman/CEO, Global Strategic Corporate Sustainability Pvt. Ltd, and Executive in Residence, INSEAD Business School

Provocateurs not Philanthropists: Turning Good Intentions into Global Impact by Manzanal-Frank is a breath of fresh air to the person who wants to make a real difference in the world of development. The book is a fresh look at organizing and running projects. Organized around 10 principles, the book shows the reader that humility shown by admitting a lack of total knowledge and accepting failure will allow a person to create true collaboration and become a provocateur. Those who have experience in the world of development and those who are just starting will appreciate this book.

Mike Schmidt, Director, Intercultural Studies Program, Prairie College

RESETTING OUR FUTURE

Provocateurs not Philanthropists

Turning Good Intentions into Global Impact

RESETTING OUR FUTURE

Provocateurs not Philanthropists

Turning Good Intentions into Global Impact

Maiden R. Manzanal-Frank

CHANGEMAKERS
BOOKS

Winchester, UK
Washington, USA

JOHN HUNT PUBLISHING

First published by Changemakers Books, 2022
Changemakers Books is an imprint of John Hunt Publishing Ltd., No. 3 East Street,
Alresford, Hampshire SO24 9EE, UK
office@jhpbooks.com
www.johnhuntpublishing.com
www.changemakers-books.com

For distributor details and how to order please visit the 'Ordering' section on our website.

Text copyright: Maiden R. Manzanal-Frank 2022

ISBN: 978 1 78904 836 0
978 1 78904 837 7 (ebook)
Library of Congress Control Number: 2022937011

All rights reserved. Except for brief quotations in critical articles or reviews, no part of this
book may be reproduced in any manner without prior written permission from the publishers.

The rights of Maiden R. Manzanal-Frank as author have been asserted in accordance
with the Copyright, Designs and Patents Act 1988.

A CIP catalogue record for this book is available from the British Library.

Design: Matthew Greenfield

UK: Printed and bound by CPI Group (UK) Ltd, Croydon, CR0 4YY
Printed in North America by CPI GPS partners

We operate a distinctive and ethical publishing philosophy in
all areas of our business, from our global network of authors to
production and worldwide distribution.

Contents

For Ty and Adriana, the greatest blessing on earth

Acknowledgements

This book would not have been conceived and completed without the support of a lot of people who provided valuable assistance, guidance, and encouragement throughout all the stages.

There was a long gestation for this book. Way back in 2005, I was with a group of young women lamenting all the wrongs we found in our journeys into development and what we could do better next time. We decided that we would no longer conform but transform our jobs and careers and pursue righteous indignation by setting a good example for others in the sector.

Before it became a book, I was toying with the idea of an ebook that I could just write and give to people who I thought would appreciate it. Never in my wildest dreams did I think of writing a commercial book. Thanks to Lynn Slobogian who read the first few pages of the ebook and made great comments for improvements.

It was only in early 2019 that I realized that, going to all these efforts, I might as well go for a commercial book. Nothing to lose, more to gain. Thanks to the book sprint workshop colleagues for the encouragement and Dr. Alan Weiss, I acknowledged that a book would be the best vehicle for ideas to spread.

It took me almost three and a half months to find the right publisher, emailing close to 60 agents and publishers in the US, Canada, and the UK, and being rejected left and right. I want to thank some of the publishers for taking the time to encourage me to continue the search even though it seemed fruitless at times.

I want to thank my passionate and patient publisher, Tim Ward, for always being on standby to clarify issues and to get me moving forward. I would like to thank Changemaker Books imprint and John Hunt for trusting in my work and ideas. For the authors in the *Resetting the Future* series, thanks for showing the way, introducing your contacts, and leaving reviews. I want to thank David Balzer for his superb editing work, Tom Bowman for the beautiful front cover design, and Hayoung Park for the graphics design.

Many people lent their time, expertise, professional skills, connections, and perspectives, namely: Dr. Ravi Fernando, Dr. Satwinder Bains, Dr. Steve Wisser, Calvin Djiofack, Cidalia Luis-Akbar, Eric Rajah, Risa Gold, Ben Hoogendoorn, Erinch Sahan, Modestus Karunaratne, and the many people who were featured in this book in many forms. Special thanks to the endorsers who took the time to read and register their appreciation. Future thanks to the readers who will leave reviews for other readers!

When I announced that I was writing a book, so many people offered to help, which is overwhelming and humbling to know. They are too many to mention, but a few people went above and beyond. My networks in Indonesia, Bangladesh, the Philippines, Sri Lanka, India, Nepal, the US, the UK, and Thailand, to name a few, offered to host my remote book launches. I would like to thank my Rotary World family, the Rotary Clubs in Central Edmonton, Calgary, and Abbotsford, British Columbia, the Rotary Peace Fellowship Program, especially the Class of 2015, the Rotary Peace Fellowship Alumni Association Officers and Regional Representatives, and the Rotary Peace Centers recently established in each region and their academic partners. To my allies at the Chulalongkorn University Rotary Center, International Studies on Peace, Conflict Transformation, and Development, thanks for all your support.

My family, Precy Reales and siblings, Atty. Dennis Manzanal, Adona Hamto, and Viscount Manzanal, thanks for all your sacrifices and unfailing love. To my nieces and nephews, thanks for spending time on Zoom with us during the lockdowns. You enriched our lives. For my super-supportive in-laws, Ken and Susan Frank, aunts and uncles, and relatives from overseas and at home, my sincere gratitude.

I thank God for blessing me with these serendipitous events and supportive characters which led me to successful publishing. To Him be the glory!

List of Abbreviations

5Ps	Purpose, Passion, Practice, Provision, Paradigm
AI	Artificial Intelligence
BC	British Columbia, Canada
CEO	Chief Executive Officer
COVID-19	Coronavirus
CSR	Corporate Social Responsibility
DEVEX	Development Exchange
HHI	Harvard Humanitarian Initiative
HIV/AIDS	Human immunodeficiency virus /Acquired immunodeficiency syndrome
ICT	Information and Communication Technology
IMF	International Monetary Fund
NASA	National Aeronautics and Space Administration
NGOs	Non-Government Organizations
RCT	Random Controlled Trial
ROE	Return on Equity
ROI	Return on Investment
TB	Tuberculosis
TED	Technology, Entertainment, Design
TV	Television
UN	United Nations
WB	World Bank

Introduction

How can you create a lasting legacy with communities, countries, families, or individuals who can benefit from your vision and action? How can you use your passion, talent, and creativity for meaningful, global impact?

You don't have to be Angelina Jolie, George Clooney, Bill Gates, or Bono.

Many impact leaders are doing great work worldwide without cameras and social media trailing their every move. They are the stay-at-home mom who organized a network of moms to promote immunization, women's health, and children's wellness in developing countries. The medical student who helped build schools in Afghanistan through the strength of her networks in Canada. The engineer who, after recovering from cancer, repaired hundreds of abandoned wells all over the world. The psychiatrist who is sustainably building a hospital in West Africa. The man who, for 60 years, donated his blood every week. The IT business owner who grew a church budget from $5,000 to $2 million to build schools and clinics in Africa and Asia. These are everyday people—professionals, store owners, entrepreneurs, carpenters—with extraordinary vision and exemplary leadership and courage. They get things done, and inspire others to do better.

Statistics merely scratch the surface. The 2022 global estimate of monthly volunteers aged 15 years and older was 824.4 million worldwide, with 61 million full-time monthly equivalent workers.[1] Out of the monthly working-age population, 14.3% volunteer informally. Women make up 53.42% of all informal volunteering. In Canada, 69 average hours per person are devoted to international volunteering every year.[2]

In the United States, the average age of someone who donates to charities is 64, a fact that will become more interesting as

10,000 Baby Boomers retire per day in the United States over the next ten years.[3] The World Bank has called the current generation "the first in history that can end extreme poverty."[4]

Small organizations, the engines of people-to-people development work, grew in the last ten years. Out of 16,000 nonprofit organizations in the United States devoted to international relief and development, 70% have a budget of USD100,000 or less.[5] In Canada, 76% of organizations with more than 30% of overseas expenditures are small organizations relying mostly on voluntary and in-kind contributions.[6]

This is a book for anyone who wants to turn their good intentions into global impact. Perhaps you are already a leader at the height of your career. Or you are an emerging leader who will become a decision-maker for companies, institutions, or public-sector bodies. Perhaps you have no organizational affiliation. The rise of the lone altruist has been a fascinating trend for the last 20 years, and it's not going away. Indeed, do-it-yourself humanitarianism is a product of our increasingly digital world.

Understanding Impact and Its Discontents

Building new infrastructure, providing training, education, or immediate relief, conducting research, overhauling public systems of care, cleaning the ocean, saving the gorillas: anything that could make a difference in the lives of people and their communities is about that elusive, multifaceted thing called impact.

Despite attempts by economists, statisticians, political scientists, sociologists, and other leading thinkers to qualify this concept, "impact" is highly political and subjective. It's partly about ideology, partly about accountability and transparency, and partly about the human quest to ensure that, at the end of the day, what we do matters. A person on their deathbed wants to know one thing: they made a difference. It doesn't matter if it's for a thousand people or one. The former would be neat, the latter, potentially, more rewarding.

I was with a team of evaluators reviewing a disaster response program in 2015. At one point, the junior member turned to the senior member and asked how many babies he had saved in his career. He'd worked with an international agency promoting children's rights and welfare worldwide but quit after a decade. For me, this was a trick question—and not a joke. To gauge someone's personal fulfillment and accomplishment, do we turn to sheer numbers? Any response short of pure heroism would have been a total disappointment.

From the point of view of institutionalists, impact can be measured quantitatively (numbers, percentage, ratios), qualitatively (change in conditions, attitudes, behaviors, mindsets, cultural preferences, levels of empowerment, agency, etc.), and via monetization. I define impact in this book by much more than the number of babies you can save or the number of wells you've built. It's about the long-lasting positive outcomes of activities and interventions in partner communities that increase their agency, self-determination, and collective capacity. More than complying with accountability, impact is an orientation and a principle to live by.

It doesn't matter how many babies you save. What matters is the extent to which your activities lead to improvements in people's conditions. How have your interventions created an environment in which people can aspire to better things for themselves and their communities? Have the results of your work proven the community could, or can now, do it on their own?

Media don't help. We have come to measure impact based on how it applies to wars, terrorism, natural disasters, and other events the media sensationalize, while completely ignoring others. News stories suggest resources and attention should be given to certain dire cases requiring an immediate, emergency, global-humanitarian response. Typhoon Haiyan in the Philippines, the refugee crisis in Yemen and among the Rohingya, and the evolving Ukraine crisis received a high level of global attention, demanding rapid political and humanitarian action, if not resolution. Research confirms that when traditional media highlight gaps in relief operations or point to the deprivation of people affected, more giving occurs, as opposed to when media are absent or underreport a situation.

The impact of everyday individuals—under-the-radar, underfunded, and underappreciated—is passed over because they're not newsworthy enough. Nothing less than a thousand beneficiaries will do for a page's worth of newspaper coverage or a few seconds on TV. I don't learn much from these bite-sized stories of success, heroism, or epic failure. They don't add up. The messiness and rollercoaster rides of the startup— the in-between truths—are more helpful and revealing.

Impact is not about a return on investment (ROI) or a return on equity (ROE) but a return on humanity (ROH), something greatly needed in a materialistic and convenience-obsessed society. After her "voluntour" in Ecuador working in a small orphanage, a friend told me she found the peace she'd always yearned for. ROH is a return to civic consciousness that transcends the narrow differences of politics, ideology, demographics, geography, and class. It's about self-fulfillment, a life of purpose, and integrated living.

The Three Types of Altruists: The Bureaucrat, the Philosopher, and the Entrepreneur

Whether you're on Wall Street or High Street, at a nonprofit, or run your own business, you're already cut out for great work. With methods and approaches you already use in problem-solving, decision-making, and managing teams, start seeing yourself as equipped to heed that "second calling." Consider the three archetypes who currently make up the global impact arena—and how they might provide inspiration for anyone with the talent, energy, and sensitivity to make a difference.

Traditional *bureaucrats* crunch the numbers, sign the reports, and throw tea parties after a day's work at ambassadors' houses. They obsess over the processes, systems, harmonization, efficiencies, and various management styles they might employ to improve their teams. No surplus or redundancy goes uninvestigated. Bureaucrats, as careerists, want to make a better world, one job, project, or budget cycle at a time.

Bob is a bureaucrat. He works 9–5 in an office in the capital for the largest development bank in the region. He takes pride in his work, mulling over a set of policy recommendations that will ultimately improve work in the field. He brings together different stakeholders to combine the best of theories, field practices, and expert opinions in a report that he hopes could spark a discussion within the agency.

Philosophers walk to the beat of a different drum. They believe social good is a matter of thinking and living. Whether through faith, ideology, or values, philosophers are forces for good because of their beliefs and conviction. Mother Teresa and Jane Goodall are our major popular culture examples: humanitarian heroes who walked the roads less traveled and told the world of the joy they found helping others. Some philosophers are unknown or forgotten, because they do not seek the limelight for themselves; instead, they live their principles daily.

Karl is a philosopher. He is a serial international volunteer who, for a decade, has worked on almost all the continents. For him this is not a phase but a lifelong calling. Without a permanent address and permanent friends, he relishes living in the now, serving others, and using his gifts and talents for photography, writing, and journalism to train local nonprofits to elevate their storytelling. His faith in humanity allows him to become a witness to the evolutions in people and organizations.

Entrepreneurs are the disrupters in social-development spaces, tirelessly bringing business wisdom to projects, ideas, and processes for massive application, which can transform societies and people for good. Using a startup, bootstrapping mentality, entrepreneurs are edgy risk-takers, comfortable with a high level of ambiguity and discomfort. They persist despite lack of support or resources, or an imminent failure to launch. They continue even when they receive backlash from traditionalists. For entrepreneurs, there is no other path to success than to rinse and repeat until something sticks. They can also measure the bottom lines, know how to scale up, and are never short of experiments.

Belinda is an entrepreneur. A business owner of a medium-sized manufacturing company, she sits on local community boards and gives to charities of her choice on a regular basis. But she doesn't just want to give money; she wants to be personally involved, using her business skills and ideas to generate new solutions. For five years, she has led relief missions to six countries in Africa and South America. She persuaded one local nonprofit to use blended finance to fund their future programs, and has convened a small network of her business partners to start thinking ahead.

You can fall into one or all of these categories. Should you take risks, be accountable, or be super-passionate? Should you dot the Is and cross the Ts or throw caution to the wind and try something messy? You could embody a multiplicity of approaches, or make your own pathway. It's up to you.

Humanitarian work is immediate, time-bound, and focused on saving lives. Development is long-term, multifaceted, and aims to eradicate the impacts of current-day social problems. Humanitarian and development arenas receive billions of dollars through aid and direct foreign investments. Organizations sponsoring, supporting, and implementing these initiatives scrutinize them through reports, measures, experiments, and evaluations to measure their impact. This book focuses on developmental impact—the long-view approach to creating the conditions for communities to be self-reliant and self-renewing. While I am not concerned with specific metrics or evaluation approaches, I try to provide perspectives that you can adapt to your own unique situations and challenges.

Conformity Hinders Impact

Rollo May said: "The enemy of courage is not cowardice but conformity."

In development, conformist thinking erodes gains from previous generations. Top-down ideology did not help Africa and other poor regions rise out of their past colonial struggles. From the green revolution to building dams, from investing in microfinance to responding to climate change, each paradigm of development—the planner, the searcher, and the experimenter, as defined by ongoing aid-industry discourse—demands questioning assumptions and received thinking. More funding for experiments that yield important insights into how people buy into a development project can help impact leaders innovate, without leaving behind the wisdom that already exists, and is still very useful.

Initiatives always come from somewhere—traditionally an academic review, a World Bank (WB) or International Monetary Fund (IMF) analysis, government policy, a significant funder's initiative. Yet rarely are the locals consulted who bear the consequences of these initiatives. Locals are often left with no choice but to accept whatever aid is sent their way, no matter its form or effectiveness. To this day, organizations seeking funding must bend backward to become grantees for many band-aid solutions. Practitioners at the lower levels get the short end of the stick most of the time.

As the grant writer for one of the Philippines' local organizations a decade ago, I had to rewrite a grant application countless times. There was an accountability checklist to cross off, research to ground the project in the larger context, fact-checking, many consultations with partners and stakeholders... On and on it went. After a few years of writing proposals, I hated fundraising, not because of the burdensome process that entailed rejections but the duplicity of putting new wine into old bottles.

The culture of playing by the rules can silence diverse views about how things should be done, especially at the local level. If local leaders think they can't disagree with those who hold power, they become detached from outcomes. Their work becomes oppressive, robotic, and ineffective. TEDx celebrities may have bright ideas, but their new approaches may disorient the very people who are supposed to implement them. For whom do development benefits accrue? What disruptions do they create? Who, ultimately, gains the most from development?

The microfinance industry, for example, thought it had the solution to mass poverty. But recent, randomized controlled trials and studies show it only resulted in modest gains to household consumption, income, and social outcomes.[7] Folly has gripped our decision-makers for many years: the search for the flashiest solution that will tide them over until another arrives. Before we know it, millions of dollars are chasing the shadows of misguided hopes.

The Provocateur

Suppose you had the diligence and managerial know-how of the bureaucrat, the purpose-filled drive of the philosopher, and the risk-taking instinct of the entrepreneur. Would you be changing the world? Would you be out there making waves?

Provocateurs are transformative leaders for today's in-flux development field. They don't have all the answers and don't keep closely held information all to themselves, a power move still prevalent in business and management roles. Provocateurs "integrate creative insight, persistence, energy, intuition, and sensitivity"[8] to get their partners moving alongside them. They are situation-as-a-whole leaders[9] because they integrate vast amounts of contextual information from their working environments to create synergies of action.

The provocateur has no need for a formal title, higher education, or a million followers. Impact is something you embody in everything you do—thoughts, words, and actions. If you are a farmer, you start helping with farming practices that are sustainable and locally appropriate. If you are a nutritionist, you implement proper nutrition for mothers and infants. If you are an accountant, you use modern practices that local organizations can adapt for their financial decision-making. There's no barrier to entry for the provocateur. Small acts of expertise go a long way.

The world is hungry for leaders who aren't delusional about fame, success, reputation, wealth, and other traps. Using the Global Leadership Impact Framework and the Ten Principles of Global Impact, you can learn how to lead with boldness, and accelerate your legacy.

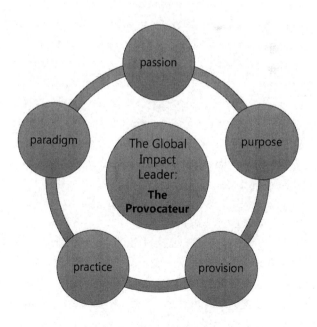

Figure 1: The Global Impact Leadership Framework

The 5Ps of the Global Impact Leadership Framework

The 5Ps of the Global Impact Leadership Framework—Purpose, Passion, Practice, Provision, and Paradigm—are essential to every provocateur.

- *Purpose* comes first. A higher purpose—a calling, a compass that's unwavering and unyielding—drives the global impact leader. Two purposes converge in the heart of the provocateur: 1) to walk among those they seek to serve; and 2) to share their purpose, realizing it together, with change partners. *Passion, Practice, and Provision without Purpose is a wannabe.*

- *Passion* fuels the purpose. Doing something meaningful requires a healthy dose of zeal. There is no such thing as a smooth ride when working in fragile situations with vulnerable populations. Passion gets you through the hard times. It's not just positive energy or unbridled enthusiasm. Passion is from the Latin word *passio*, which means "to suffer." For me, such suffering means having patience, perseverance, generosity, dedication, understanding, empathy, resilience, and selflessness. The road will be treacherous and unpredictable. Selflessness shouldn't mean martyrdom, denying yourself for the sake of others. You want to live longer, wiser, and healthier so you can serve better, but sacrifice is certainly important. *Purpose, Practice, and Provision without Passion is a paycheck.*

- *Practice* is the stuff global impact leaders are made of. Practice is your communion: day-to-day actions that allow you to achieve your objectives. Yes, practice makes perfect. Without action, the provocateur becomes part of the problem rather than the solution. Practice perfects your purpose and sharpens your passion. *Purpose, Passion, and Provision without Practice is a dilettante.*

- *Provision* calls the provocateur's heart, mind, and soul to the actual task. It brings together all the tools and mechanisms needed to thrive: natural gifts, talents, competencies, traits, networks, resources, and any other means necessary to bring impact to life. Provision depends on intelligence to determine what matters and what can be used to get the best results. It also requires imagination: thinking through what can be used to bring communities, societies, technologies, and systems into new ways of being, doing, working, and coexisting. *Purpose, Passion, and Practice without Provision is an idealist.*

- The *Paradigm* that encircles this framework makes purpose, passion, practice, and provision work together, to create impact. A correct paradigm can make purpose, passion, practice, and provision reinforce one another, turning your mandate into a dynamic, reiterative process. The paradigm is important because it doesn't assume a beginning or ending. Rather, it invites conversations about turns and pivots along the road. Without a paradigm, your purpose, passion, provision, and practice are directionless—vulnerable to personal whims, and to ethical or professional mistakes.

The 5Ps in Practice: My Story, and Lisa's

Like many of us, I started out as a 9–5 jobber and idealist. I wanted to travel and see the world. But I wanted to be useful as well. A former professor asked me what my ambition was, and I told him I wanted to work for one of the most prestigious international organizations in the world. "That's easy," he said. What he meant was that it was easy to get into the organization, but much harder to stay the course and make a difference.

My career didn't work out the way I thought. I joined several local nonprofit organizations one at a time, doing project management, advocacy, research, conducting training and skills-building, writing grants, building networks and communities of practice, traveling nonstop in remote, far-flung areas with international partners. It was exhilarating and disappointing at the same time. I also volunteered with an international organization that brought me face to face with other juniors doing the same things.

After years of working in the development sector, I was frustrated. Leaders in the organizations I worked with acted like they owned the show. There was no accountability or ethics when it came to working and showing tangible outcomes. When funding got tough, they resorted to chasing money for flavor-of-the-month projects. I didn't feel there was a future for me in development unless I learned what others were doing successfully on an international level.

I faced similar issues and dilemmas for the first five years in different nonprofit organizations. As I compared notes and talked to various young people working at multiple operational levels, they all had a lot of things to say that resonated with me. It wasn't that the development sector wasn't robust, professional, and dynamic. Even influential organizations were saddled with larger issues professionals like us simply had to accept as a harsh reality. Donor dependency, mission and scope creep, and financial instability created a subculture of impoverished leaders incapable of nurturing the next generation in the field.

As a practitioner and observer in the global-impact field since 2001, I have witnessed large and small organizations achieve great feats and suffer monstrous failures. Some achievements have merited global attention and admiration from various sectors. These organizations appear to have found the proverbial "success formula," while most organizations seem to have gotten lost in the haze of productivity and the strive for legitimacy: a good thing until it becomes the sole driver for transformation. Productivity doesn't mean you're achieving your outcomes. Legitimate organizations often produce only piecemeal results.

For many years I searched high and low for what individual champions can use as evergreen principles—ones that do not lose relevance when new, shiny topics arise. I was able to observe closely through employment, volunteering, consultancy, training, and teaching how these time-tested insights make sense even to those who do not have the parachute of larger organizations or massive online communities. It all boils down to leadership playing a significant role in achieving global impact. Fortunately, it doesn't reside in large institutions and human resource departments but in individuals already committed to this undertaking—the doers, not the planners, managers, and experts.

What does a doer look like? Consider Lisa. One day, Lisa's friend Janet called her after visiting Bangladesh. Janet was ecstatic to tell her all about what they were doing in the orphanage near Cox's Bazar. The orphanage was in dire need of a daycare centre, a school, and lodging facilities for those who were visiting and volunteering with the organization. Janet asked Lisa to help them fundraise, with the goal of growing a seed fund of at least USD50,000 for the next two years. Lisa, an accountant in her small town who traveled very little, did not know what to do. She went to a fundraising event organized by Janet and met some community members from the Bangladeshi diaspora. She decided this was a worthy cause. For two years, Lisa helped Janet fundraise, and shared her networks.

When an opportunity to join Janet on a trip to Bangladesh came up, Lisa looked forward to meeting the leaders of the orphanage and seeing firsthand the realities they were facing. Armed with optimism and her accounting lens, Lisa saw how the orphanage not only needed a building to house several facilities, but also a sustainable financial foundation. She told the leaders to get themselves local financial advisors who could professionalize their bookkeeping and accounting. She also told the Executive Director to monitor their cash flow and insisted on hiring someone every year to audit their books. The trip was an eye-opening experience. Lisa found she could really contribute her own expertise and talent, beyond asking her friends for donations.

In her conversation with Janet and some colleagues, Lisa determined the orphanage needed to have a nonprofit in Canada that could help build capacities on a long-term basis. After three years, Lisa, Janet, and other Canadian friends started a nonprofit called "Bright Hope Society" that aimed to partner with orphanage organizations in developing countries, particularly in South Asia and Southeast Asia, where girls are the most vulnerable to abuse and violence. Janet became the organization's first part-time Executive Director, while the rest of the Canadians provided volunteer hours, including Lisa.

Lisa saw an opportunity to help the finance board member from the local counterpart think about sustainability. In a series of workshops she facilitated, Lisa helped create a sustainable business model for the daycare, school, and lodging facility that funded their operational costs. As the orphanage grew in size and operations, Lisa knew it needed to build strong partnerships with local government and agencies—this time, not in a siloed way, but to leverage the orphanage's growing influence in its own communities and beyond. The partnership with the local orphanage ended in a five-year agreement, which included broad stakeholder engagement to ensure the success of new enterprises once their support ended.

Looking back at what she had accomplished as a volunteer and leader, Lisa recognized that she never imposed her own model on the communities with whom she had worked. To enrich them, she facilitated the process in which local leaders could think differently to improve governance and become better stewards. Her advice to aspiring impact leaders is to always be open-minded with every action. Help the people help themselves.

Ten Principles for Global Impact

A wise person learns from the mistakes of others. Professional organizations and individual actors make many wasteful mistakes because altruism alone doesn't work. We need a blueprint, a roadmap, for those who want to learn more about helping that works. Altruism without the principles and systems that bind the doer to their work and assign value to impacts is useless.

The Ten Principles for Global Impact provide you with practical advice to accelerate your legacy in your chosen partner community. They help you avoid pitfalls along the way, saving thousands of dollars, hours of time, and precious talent. They also challenge you to think outside the box, whether you are dependent on or independent of a larger organization.

- *Principle 1: Do Better Than No Harm.* This explains how to avoid doing harm on the ground by improving communities based on what you find there.
- *Principle 2: Forge Strong Bonds with Your Change Partner.* This is all about enlivening change partners through community engagement.
- *Principle 3: Play the Long Game.* This principle elucidates the need for effectiveness by asking the right questions.
- *Principle 4: Learn from Mistakes.* This principle informs you that mistakes can guide actions and provide the impetus for improvements. You can learn from your mistakes, and even better, from the mistakes of others.
- *Principle 5: Access Your Ignorance and Borrow Shamelessly.* This principle encourages you to embrace failures and use ambiguity as a starting point for greater success, to cultivate innovation.

- *Principle 6: Don't Underestimate Your Impact.* This principle is about the impact-orientation in your practice. The provocateur should strive to be effective and waste-free.
- *Principle 7: Empower Your Defenders through Your Story.* This principle asserts the power of your story to build up your defenders who will go the extra mile for your impact.
- *Principle 8: Envision the End You Intend.* This principle reminds you to work with a farewell in mind, to enrich and sustain your relationships and undertakings.
- *Principle 9: Find and Nurture Your Community.* This principle is about marshaling the resources you need to build community and inspire others with your work.
- *Principle 10: Dare the Impossible.* It is all about finding better ideas in unlikely or even under-resourced places and bringing innovation to the margins.

All these principles, motivated by the 5Ps, Purpose, Passion, Provision, Practice, and Paradigm, represent a call to action—a strategic manifesto for the provocateur.

These Ten Principles come from my experience working in the Global South. They debunk myths and assumptions, turn conventional wisdom on its head, and expose gaps in our actions.

Presented in a conversational, reader-friendly tone, this book distills insights I've collected over the years, from my observations and experiences working in national, regional, and global organizations. My formative years working with marginalized populations such as artisans, cooperatives, farmers' networks, and grassroots groups were pivotal. My subsequent consulting work, focused on local and global on-purpose organizations in Canada and overseas, confirmed some of the insights of those years. This book uses narrative inquiry, document analysis, and interviews with impact leaders, thought leaders, and practitioners in impact and sustainability. Each principle cites real-life cases that demonstrate the challenges and future of global impact work. At the end of each chapter/ principle, there are summary questions that help busy readers reflect on their journey.

Although this book stresses time-honored approaches to global-development leadership, it also contributes to implementation science in the field, acknowledging the emergence of new actors who are hands-on, tech-savvy, and increasingly impact-oriented. Some are non-Western, faith-based, and diaspora-led. None come from the molds of traditional philanthropy. They are neither billionaires nor pseudo-humanitarian cyber-clones. Propelled by the globalization of media and digital platforms, these new altruists are driven more by their morals, passions, and self-fulfillment than by a mistaken concept of needy Others.

While, as I have mentioned, Internet-based platforms can impede true global impact, digital culture is also directing people across the globe to give to worthy causes. Direct payments can be sent by a click to anywhere in the world—to a woman in Nepal raising two goats, for example, or a shoemaker in Nigeria who needs a few hundred as a loan to scale his business.

The opportunities to do great work are vast. COVID-19 has exposed significant fault lines in the politics of global health, including the hemorrhaging of economies and the mental-health suffering of millions during lockdown. Significant issues concerning vaccine cost and availability, and strategies for strengthening public health systems across the world, demand more than knee-jerk, protectionist, blame-game reactions. More than ever, the current global pandemic recovery requires a serious, holistic rethink of how we can do good, better. For whom, and by what standards, do we commit ourselves to positive change?

To bastardize a saying sometimes attributed to Churchill: "Never waste a good crisis." The COVID-19 lockdowns gave me an extraordinary, once-in-a-lifetime impetus to conduct research and write this book. The pandemic was a great excuse to engage a broader audience in conversations about individual and collective responsibility for our planet, the world's health, and our future prosperity.

Whether you are leading teams in the boardroom or thinking about your next big, world-changing idea—this book is for you. You want the adventure and challenge of bringing your ideas to life, and of achieving realistic impacts as your legacy. It's time to learn first-rate lessons and make them work—on the ground, not just in fine print. A movement of provocateurs capable of extraordinary impact is underway. Join them in making meaningful change a reality.

Principle 1

Do Better Than No Harm

The first principle for global impact leaders is inspired by the Hippocratic Oath: do better than no harm. As with the Oath, there is a consensus in development that we should not harm those we are trying to serve. While the practice of accountability takes care of this in operational ways, doing harm by thinking you know it all and then doing nothing is the contemporary version of doing harm. Given the need out there, however, stopping in your tracks because you're afraid of doing harm is not an option. To avoid both misadventure and paralysis, you must investigate your paradigms and begin to see yourself as a provocateur, not a hero or a philanthropist.

My first encounter with development started when I was in grade school, living in an impoverished area in Pasig, Metro Manila. A neighbor approached my grandmother with the possibility of getting sponsored by a family in the United States. If my family couldn't support my (and my three other siblings') schooling, an organization could send money for supplies and allowance. In return, I would write cards and send photos detailing my academic progress. Soon enough, news spread about the sponsorship. A few weeks later, the neighbor told my grandmother that we had to go on a waitlist because of overwhelming demand from the community. Disappointed, my grandmother retorted, "Forget about it."

My story is an example of the impact of a certain kind of aid in one community, benefiting only a few households and discouraging most others. The perception of distribution inequity lingered in people's minds. Negative public perceptions weakened community support.

Everyone feels impact differently. Taking time to consider

how helping can lead to harm is an important way to question major assumptions you make about the value of help, and the mechanisms used to give help. Which group should be helped? What constitutes good, safe, sustainable help? What measures do you use to make sure the help is real and felt? There are moral, political, social, cultural, economic, and psychological impacts of aid and services that everyone who wants to help needs to understand. Something that might be valuable to one group of beneficiaries could easily have unintended consequences for others. This book provides a general perspective on impact, results orientation, and effectiveness.

Doing Harm by Knowing It All

Knowing-it-all assumes a superior point of view, methodology, technology, product, or service, and does not consider the contexts of people in the change process. Call it colonialist, supremacist, imperialist, or other names. Knowing-it-all involves a subjective judgment—an opinion passed off as truth—that makes objects out of those Others who are presumed to need help. People with a know-it-all attitude have no regard for how people interpret their own lives with their own meanings.

My illiterate grandmother was a much sought-out advisor in our neighborhood. From marital conflicts, drug addiction, petty crimes, wayward children, and unplanned pregnancies, she helped our neighbors mediate their squabbles or resolve their issues with practical advice. She was nine years old when World War II broke out in the Philippines, and the Japanese occupied Manila for three years. With her younger siblings in tow, she had to evacuate all of them before the Japanese could take them as prisoners or subjugated civilians. With her wisdom and ability to read into people, she was the best informal, influential leader the neighborhood ever had.

Many homegrown talents and wisdom found in communities

do not fit Western standards but work just fine in their own contexts. That people who need outside help are damaged, that they would likely trade everything to become someone in the developed world, is a gross misconception. Most of the time, it's not lack of money or agency that's the problem but a scarcity mentality. It can be debilitating when people believe that they do not have options to act in their own best interests due to prolonged deprivation.

I once gave a presentation to a service club from West Africa on implementing and fundraising for an international project. One member remarked, "You are talking as if everything goes well together here, [that] the electricity, the roads, the Internet are all working perfectly." I responded, "It's difficult, but you have options, brains, talents, gifts, networks—you have a lot. Don't discount it." He became quiet. Nothing is as paralyzing as having the scarcity mindset when opportunities and resources can still be creatively leveraged, even in starkly depressed conditions.

In 2010, Jason Sadler, a successful American businessman, attempted to send one million T-shirts to Africa.[1] He wanted to help, but his methods and ideas were misguided. A young woman on her first trip to the Gambia brought a lot of used clothes in her luggage to give away as a donation. She found out that it's better to help the local textile economy instead. Sending rubber shoes or teddy bears as donations to a disaster area is counterproductive; evidence shows that cash donations are better than physical goods.

There are many well-meaning Jasons out there who lack understanding of the complex issues facing a region or a particular country or community. Upon reflection and discussion with wise, local advisors, and after much online criticism, Jason withdrew his campaign and helped select nonprofits with social media supports that were tied directly to his business.

Doing Nothing Versus Doing Something for Optics

Doing nothing in the face of injustice and inequality is the worst form of subterfuge. The 1994 Rwandan genocide is a classic example of a time when the international community pretended that an atrocity wasn't happening, excused itself from what was dismissed as a "domestic issue," and later washed its hands of taking responsibility for the collective trauma and horror.

Doing nothing at the micro-level is also about having blinders on, and includes compartmentalizing certain development areas that hold more promise for funders to support. Some efforts take a long time with no real immediate gains. Sometimes, no parties are willing to co-share the costs and risks of projects. It may look like things are working well on the surface, but nothing has moved on a deeper level. Many projects are picked and chosen based on convenience, speed, and demonstrable traction, to show the world (or the investors), "Look, we've done it. Now, let's move on and ask for more funding."

A year and a half ago, while I was cruising down Central Alberta roads, I saw about a hundred international flags dotting the highway. Local charity groups had organized this display for veterans, to commemorate their legacies. This public-recognition gesture had no real, tangible value. Commuters didn't care, or want to be distracted while driving. After two weeks, strong winds battered the flags. Some became bent, and some totally disappeared. Good intentions didn't even last a month.

In 2020 the local government of the City of Manila drew criticisms for its beach-enhancement project, which transported dolomite, a white material used to replenish beach sand, to the tune of P28 million. A scientist from the University of the Philippines noted that during high tide and storms, the material can be washed out and dispersed, with adverse environmental effects. Mining of dolomite was subsequently banned in the area that had been used to source it for the beach.[2]

Be a Provocateur, not a Hero or a Philanthropist

Heroes and saints are gone and done, the products of old paradigms. Heroes miss out on impacts because they typically do everything unilaterally and sacrificially. Bureaucrats, philosophers, and entrepreneurs get caught up in their bubble, unable to provide the lateral leadership needed to effect change at the systemic level.

Mother Teresa was a saint; others tried to emulate her but failed. This is a *set-up-to-fail* paradigm, where only a few people come out of it healthier and more robust. If you must give up everything to pursue your life's work, then it's usually not worth pursuing. A zero-sum existence is romantic but, in practice, deeply flawed. The infamous story of mountaineer-turned-humanitarian Greg Mortensen, author of *Three Cups of Tea*, who was exposed for his misuse of fundraising money, teaches lessons about the damage that can be done by a hero complex, considering the realities of running a successful charity organization, and responding adequately to demands for accountability and truthfulness.

Provocateurs are not saints or heroes. They are regarded as rowdy, divisive troublemakers. With the right stimuli and orientation, provocateurs can shift some of our paradigms and challenge our thinking, by working on the ground with people. Because they have notoriety, expecting neither love nor adoration, they have nothing to lose. We think we know the provocateur: in organizations, "intrapreneurs"; in lifestyle settings, "enlightened vagabonds"; in corporate environments, the "next Steve Jobs"; or, in faith-based settings, "truth-tellers." But these are pseudo-provocateurs. It's up to you to find and nurture a real provocateur in your team or organization. Or to become one, if you want to make a compelling difference.

Philanthrocapitalism[3] is on the rise. Icons and billionaires are espousing a different kind of philanthropy: market-based, capitalist, and for-profit. These actors handle their investments personally. Critics argue that this form of "free gift"[4] philanthropy masks self-interest and corporate agendas. With lack of accountability, such entities can easily dominate the world stage, their powers unchecked by any government or multilateral institution. The Gates Foundation funded 10% (at USD531M) of the World Health Organization's (WHO) budget from 2008 to 2019,[5] an unprecedented move in the WHO's history. Initiatives like this favor the private sector's role in delivering goods and services, which could diminish the part traditionally played by states and nonprofit organizations.

Don't confuse the provocateur with such philanthropists. The two aren't even playing the same game. Without a doubt, provocateurs are game-changers. But they do not combine fame and fortune with doing good to absolve their guilt.

While our concept of due diligence in harm mitigation tends to stress conscientiousness and mindfulness, it also involves not listening to everything you're told. As a *provocateur, you must turn conventional wisdom, which, in fact, often does harm, upside down.*

Some myths the provocateur debunks include:

- *The best practice is out there. Find it and apply it to your situation.* Best practice starts with whatever practice and knowledge base you have. In any team, group, or community, there's always a group of people doing better than others. Investigate success, support it, and use this recipe for others to learn from and adopt.
- *Follow the trends — cryptocurrency, drones, big data — and splatter them across your key implementation strategies if possible.* Going after trends will lessen your impact.
- *The answer lies in the communities.* If they knew the answer, they wouldn't be talking to you. They don't know everything, and the fact that they're learning from you and you're learning from them becomes the catalyst for change.
- *Build a nonprofit charity if you have a goal to capture bigger*

dollars and impacts. A more significant result doesn't necessarily require a large nonprofit whose main task is to fundraise, support its own infrastructure, and build public relations.

- *Give money, and it will solve the problem.* Money on its own seldom solves the problem. Consider the unrepaired wells all over Africa.

- *Focus on the neediest.* The poorest of the poor don't need a thousand ways to survive and improve. They need one single application that will stick over time and result in breakthroughs.

- *Data will solve the problem.* Digitizing your approach doesn't deal with impact at all. It's about the people who are using the data.

- *Spend 90% of your budget on operations and 10% on administration.* Investing in organizational and program development is the wisest investment you can make to ensure your long-term viability.

Avoid Harm and Other Misadventures by Understanding Your Paradigms

In 2005, when terrorists bombed a Madrid train, I got stranded for nine hours in Charles de Gaulle Airport en route to Buenos Aires. I arrived at 8:00 a.m. and discovered I would depart as late as 10:30 p.m.

As a single woman from the Philippines traveling alone on the way to a conference meeting in Argentina, I seemed suspect. The incident happened after 9/11, when airport and border security were exceptionally tight. Two airport officials led me to a small room and one by one took items out of my carry-on bag. They asked the usual: "Where are you going?" "Why are you traveling alone?" "What's the agenda of the meeting?" "Do you have conference papers or documents to show?" I told them I was from the Philippines. The other officer countered, "I know the Philippines. I've been to Boracay." He concluded to the other officer: "She's all right. She's not a terrorist." Case closed.

Because of the positive bias toward Filipinos and that officer's lived experience on the beaches of Boracay, I didn't have to go through too much of an ordeal. Our understanding of different groups, individuals, countries, and more constitutes various interpretations of reality—paradigms. Filipinos, stereotyped as sweet human beings, are sold in Spain as a chocolate-covered biscuit brand.[6] Many Western people think that Africa is a country and that Fiji must be paradise.

When do paradigms rob us of the power to create significant impact, and do harm? We give our money, time, talents, resources, purchasing power, and everything else we've got to what we presume is a noble cause. Yes, everyone in development arguably starts out this way. But this benevolence—full of prejudice and assumption—seldom gets to the root cause of the problem. It's a great start but never sufficient—a band-aid solution that may alleviate suffering for a short time, until complex issues undercut any meaningful gain.

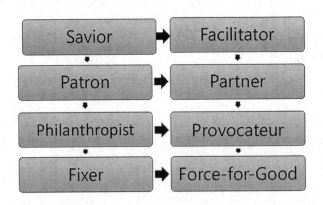

Figure 2: Paradigms In and Paradigms Out

As illustrated in Figure 2, it is better to become a *facilitator* instead of a savior, where your relationship with the change partner brings creative solutions through insights into their unique situation. Instead of being a patron, with the ability to unlock resources or connections, strive instead to become a transformative *partner*. Principle 3 discusses how genuine partnerships can increase the sustainability of results on the ground. Many successful people would like to be philanthropists. It's a feel-good label. However, this impulse should instead give way to being a *provocateur*. As a catalyst for new ideas, your significant contribution is not wealth, possessions, or connections, but your ability to influence your collaborators to think differently and act innovatively. Last, instead of thinking of yourself as a fixer, aspire to become a *force for good*, wherever you are. This will drive paradigm shifts in people's minds and hearts.

Most inscrutable problems are structural and systemic. They require different and varied approaches with actors at the national, regional, and international levels. There's a tendency to focus on physical and tangible projects: build an NGO, a well, a school, a dam, an orphanage, a clinic, a hospital, housing, training centers, a business, an app, a drone, an incubator, a lab, and so on. Many wells are built and abandoned in disrepair in developing countries. Many schools close because the community and government can't keep up with the costs of maintaining another school or hiring more teachers and training them. Some apps don't work because Internet access is still prohibitively expensive and unstable in depressed areas. Microfinance projects go bankrupt because they can't keep up with non-payments, and local actors rescinded their commitments. Businesses face red tape and corruption, from filing their certificates to getting a license for this or that. Micro-entrepreneurship programs fail to launch without government or private sector partnerships and subsidies. All of these are examples of ill-conceived solutions that bring harm.

The celebrated notion of "build philanthropism," with a focus on hammer-to-nail solutions, does not account for these challenges. Ultimately, if you are humble enough to seek wisdom in local contexts and increase your knowledge, your rate of success goes up. You can reframe solutions that restore people's self-sufficiency and strength. This is possible only through paradigm shifts, which can result in advances on several fronts.

Eric Rajah and Brian Leavitt, co-founders of A Better World, a humanitarian organization in Central Alberta, started in 1990 with a $5000 church budget for a humanitarian project. Today, they have projects in over 15 countries and have invested over $34 million in clean water, essential healthcare, quality education, sustainable agriculture, and income generation.[7] After the first five years of work in Kenya, where $10,000 funded a project, they realized that traditional philanthropic actions do not work. They used a holistic community-development model where opportunities in jobs, education, and healthcare could grow. Their goal is to ensure their partner communities' projects become permanently independent, inviting local governments and communities to contribute to costs and develop long-term local management plans. Every day, with each community partner, they are closer to meeting this goal.

Your focus should be on *doing better*. Interrogate your paradigm and decide in favor of transformation. This mental rewiring will require not just note-taking, but serious soul-searching.

The rest of this book illustrates how these shifts happen on the ground, for real-life global impact leaders.

Summary:
Reflective Questions Using the Global
Impact Leadership Framework

In the space below, reflect on the questions using the 5Ps: Purpose, Passion, Provision, Practice, and Paradigm. Remember that the 5Ps are the criteria by which you can do better and avoid harm as a global impact leader.

• What's your specific development paradigm? Write down what comes to mind, and how your paradigm should relate to doing better and avoiding harm.

• Recall instances when your work aligned with some of the pitfalls mentioned in this chapter. What lessons did you learn from your experience?

• What would you do better as a provocateur with the right paradigm? How could this paradigm shape those with whom you work, practically or organizationally, and those whose lives you intend to change for the better?

Principle 2

Forge Strong Bonds with Your Change Partner

The second principle for global impact leaders is to forge partnerships with the people who are the subject of your development project. Strengthen the power that resides within them. You must know your value, your partner, and your outcomes beforehand. Foster a relationship rooted in mutual trust, and benefits will accrue. Over time, your connection with a community will grow based on the shared purpose you hold together. When things fall apart, check your process, and take valuable lessons from the experience.

Calvin Djiofack is the hereditary king of his village in Melouong, West Cameroon. For years, the issue of clean water was a major concern for the villagers, for which the government could not provide a solution. The villagers asked him and his elders to provide piped water. He left the village to work as an economist for the World Bank but promised them that their hope would become a reality.

Fast forward: one day in October 2018, Calvin Djiofack received an email from his colleagues back home. A thousand people—women, men, youth, children, and the elderly—had lined up and dug out the main roads, up to 4km, to install pipes for the village water supply system. Community leaders had asked residents and other villagers, "Would you allow the next rain to close the holes dug by your parents or would you rather contribute to installing pipes for the water supply?" Financial support for the project came primarily from the network of community associations in the city and diaspora groups based in Europe. After one week, they received enough support for 400 meters of pipes. They had 1000 meters by the second month.

In August 2019, 5000 meters of water pipes covered the primary and secondary roads. To cover the 50% estimated costs assigned to labor, the people did all the work.

It wasn't a straightforward journey. In the dynamic agricultural community of Melouong, water sources are being depleted because of population increase and climate change. Forced to travel more than 5km to buy clean water, most people were resigned to living with minimal water access and unsafe water quality. For years, the local government had failed to act on its promise to provide a clean water supply. With the help of their traditional leaders and Djiofack, this became a reality.[1]

Today, one thousand households benefit from the water supply in Melouong. They pay their water bills consistently. Elders used the same success formula to build community solar energy, set up an education fund, and improve the commercial viability of their agri-businesses. Djiofack attributed this success to a paradigm shift: the people no longer think the government and foreign donors are the only ones who can solve these huge problems. Crucially, this shift came from traditional leaders, whom he calls the "existing structure of trust." Relying on the positive aspects of the community's culture became the key to fostering ownership and accountability.

This is not a new concept. Partnership with the people was the mantra of previous generations. Given the persistence of colonialist and imperialist notions, some scholars doubted the possibility of a genuine partnership between the Global North and South. Others noted the difference between "people power" and the power that comes from working *with* people.

From the late 1980s to the early 2000s, the people's power revolution toppled authoritarian regimes in Manila, Budapest, Warsaw, and across Latin America. Bloodless regime changes gave rise to democracies, which led to increased civic participation and a focus on good governance and moral recovery. Vibrant civil societies are responsible for the robust development landscape we see today. However, the politics of goons, guns, and gold have in some cases eroded these advances. Fragile democracies have become all too common in developing economies, with considerable gaps in citizen access to development agendas.

The Global Impact Leadership Framework locates the agency behind any partnership with the people. Amid the social turmoil and economic crises in many developing nations, the need to zero in on the value proposition, the change partner, and the assumptions behind the desired results on the ground is mission-critical.

A partnership relationship starts with understanding yourself, and being clear about your intentions. Power to the people is empowerment *with*, *through*, and *by* them. Transformative relationships are based on respect, trust, mutual understanding, and joint exploration. Without these, things could unravel overnight.

Before you pack your bags and decide to commit to doing something with a specific community, test yourself with these questions:

- Your Value Proposition: *What is the problem, the existing gaps, and the proposed solution to the identified problem?* The answer is your promise to your change partner, a statement of intent and benefits. You communicate and deliver based on this value.
- The Change Partner: *Who exactly are you trying to serve?* A rural village differs from an urban community. An international NGO is distinct from a local Rotary Club. Even in the development space, NGOs specialize in a single issue or have multiple mandates. Choosing a partner based on needs alone will get you into trouble, because there will be an overabundance of need that you can never fill. Determine your change partner based

on your value proposition and the impact you want to achieve. Choose them as diligently as the charity you donate to, or the person you elect into public office. Can you trust them with your time and money? If you have doubts, take a step back and probe.

- The Impact: *What are your outcome commitments, at the beginning, not the end?* Systemic challenges call for a systemic evaluation of impacts with different partners, at different levels, with varying degrees of significance. Failures and misfires occur because impact is an afterthought. I attended a Rotary Club meeting a few years ago. The reporter said, "We raised $125,000 for five years to build wells and schools in Namibia." Outstanding work. "We did it! Now, let's have lunch." Inputs like this fundraising sum are not tangible outcomes: the transformation you want to see with the wells and the schools. Principle 3 discusses effectiveness and the long game. Principle 7 focuses on creating a robust impact explanation for your work.

Figure 3: Impact-Focused Theory of Change

Your Theory on How and Why Change Happens

The Theory of Change,[2] used predominantly by purpose-driven organizations, describes causal links between inputs, outputs, and outcomes in the short, mid, and long terms. It provides a robust approach to ensuring impacts are well-defined, articulated, measured, and followed through the impact chain. Social projects employ the Theory of Change widely in designing, monitoring, evaluating, and reporting outcomes. Assumptions populate the logic chain to account for conditions that would enable or hinder the achievement of outcomes.

For impact leaders doing grassroots and micro work, it's important to understand the mechanisms used to harvest and measure outcomes. This provides clarity on the big whys of your actions. If you partner with a nonprofit or government institution, ask for their Theory of Change. Partner only if you're satisfied they recognize the value of this practice and implement it consistently. Your time and effort are worth investing in projects with a sound logic chain.

This chain should follow an IF–THEN–BECAUSE pattern: IF we provide community education on nutrition to breastfeeding mothers with children below five years of age, THEN these mothers can transfer this knowledge to everyday practices to ensure the health and well-being of their families and children, preventing child malnutrition and morbidity—BECAUSE they have the information to address these issues at the household and community levels.

We live in an era where we can be anywhere. But we still make decisions alongside our change partners. Be transparent about the results of your actions. There should be no maybes. Realistic actions on the ground call for a sensible logic of change.

Honest-to-Goodness Partnership with the People

A real partnership is equal and respectful, moving toward a shared purpose that will stand the test of time. You have their backs, and they have yours.

Beware of dependency and power imbalance. As a standard procedure, you must have buy-in from the community. Build a trusting connection to help them rise above challenges and think creatively. Who are the brokers and mediators? What are the structures of trust that have been present in communities for generations?

Your time with a community is very short, but could be transformational. Keep an open mind and be modest about your ideas. No visitor can replace a fully functioning community member who has knowledge, language, and social capital. Your walk with the poor and marginalized is serious business. Be humble.

Nowadays, nonprofits credit private investors and donors as their clients, because they're the funders. This approach abandons what charity is all about, peddling aid as an investment product, and stroking individual egos.

We need to return to the people, the real heroes of this narrative. The locus of transformation lies in communities. Your investments should go to them, including any praise or recognition of the project's eventual success.

Consultation, Collaboration, Partnership, Community

Being in a community is a position of strength, trust, and mutual care. A shared purpose is the glue that makes the relationship stick. Let four relational dynamics guide your work:

1. *Consultation*: Impact leaders must consult community partners for input, and invite their participation. The impact leader should assume all responsibilities and risks.
2. *Collaboration*: Impact leaders and community partners are co-planners and co-doers. Each brings value to the table, yet one party is ultimately responsible for it.
3. *Partnership*: Impact leaders and community partners are responsible for successes and failures. They jointly commit to a shared purpose. Beyond transaction, they rely on one another for support and encouragement.
4. *Community*: Belonging in a community with the partner provides a sense of purpose and protection. The community owns the results and is accountable for long-term benefit maintenance. An impact leader can evolve as a friend, advisor, confidant, and loyal supporter. Principle 8 is about evolving roles available after a successful exit.

In Melouong, traditional leaders pushed the improbable into the possible. The community did it themselves. This is genuine people power. Unless community leaders own their purpose and exercise accountability, meaningful impacts become convoluted. Sometimes they don't take root.

Some impact leaders remain at a partnership level that serves their purpose, while others move toward deeper collaboration. Whatever the case, when it's time to leave, the impact leaders are happy to go, knowing the community can sustain what they've started. When both parties commit to being co-travelers on a development journey, it leads to a trusting friendship.

Everyone who wants to help should aspire to the highest calling. Are communities better off after your involvement, or are they more dependent? Being in community with the people means assisting them to unleash their potential and realize they have it all, after all.

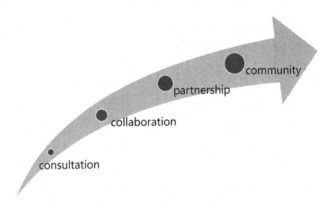

Figure 4: The Continuum of People Partnership

When Things Fall Apart, Don't Play the Blame Game

When things fall apart, the blame game happens, and you'll be tempted to determine whose fault it is. Instead of this, attack the cause of the breakdown ruthlessly through these questions:

1. Was there an actual agreement reached about the project, or merely a shallow acceptance? What evidence is there to support the former?
2. Was there a genuine consultation, or was it a perfunctory ritual, devoid of substance and vibrancy? Do you have evidence to support either?
3. Were you and your partners committed to transparent and ethical behavior? Is there consistent application of these principles in all aspects of your and/or their efforts?
4. Was there valid participation from all stakeholders? Whose opinion was given more weight? Who are the informal leaders and backers in the community? Without their support, will things move? Who are the resisters? What power do they hold?
5. Have you made your case clear about the tangible benefits the community will receive? What would be the sticking point for not going along?

In 2014, I was part of an assessment team in the Philippines monitoring a reconstruction program after Typhoon Haiyan. One day, my colleague and I went to one village and investigated the case of the "jersey can." The villagers opined that jersey cans and other relief goods received from a large organization ended up in households with less damage and less hardship than others. To them, this issue was worth reporting. My colleague went to the farthest part of the neighborhood, which took up most of his time in the area. He rejoined me on the balcony of a household. After a few minutes, he became fidgety. He asked me why we were not moving to the next location. I said, "The owner of the house went out to get snacks." I told him to be a pleasant guest. He exuded discomfort. People could read him like a book. I told him that if he was uncomfortable, people would think that their hospitality wasn't enough for him.

Resistance is better than apathy. With resistance, perhaps you can counter valid reasons with those of your own. Build trust, even if it takes years to get things going. Remember: trust is an action word. The product based on trust will speak for itself. Seek consensus, not unanimity. If a community is difficult at the initial stage, expect more problems down the road.

Partnership with the people is the practical application of your passion, purpose, provision, and paradigm. After determining the right paradigm, you will realize that a partnership is not a duty to uphold but a joy to fulfill. Reviving the people's dormant power is your greatest partnership outcome. Be careful in orchestrating your process. Be mindful of the evolving nature of your partnership. It's absolutely necessary.

Timing is everything. In the next principle, I discuss the need to prepare for the long game.

Summary:
Reflective Questions on Using the Global Impact Leadership Framework

In the space below, reflect on the questions using the 5Ps: Purpose, Passion, Provision, Practice, and Paradigm. Remember, you can use the 5Ps to empower your community partners to harness their innate strengths and capacities.

- How does a sound value statement and a robust Theory of Change help you to partner effectively and ethically with marginalized communities?

- As a global impact leader, how can you begin to see the communities you work with as the site of transformation you seek? What don't you know and what can you learn from communities?

- Relationships evolve and grow, or become stagnant and die. What challenges do you face in fostering a partnership based on a continuum of growth?

Principle 3

Play the Long Game

The third principle for global impact leaders is to play the long game by asking the right questions, which requires a laser-like focus on effectiveness. Getting results could take a lifetime of work, or it could be a clear, targeted few months or years. We tend to measure the wrong things and expect to move mountains. Real effectiveness is when you get closer to the problem: you listen to it, smell it, taste it, and get dirty. You don't fixate on diagnosis but on trial and error. Real effectiveness not only answers "What results?" but also "So what?" and "Now what?"

Trends in Effectiveness

As a global impact leader, you should understand that effectiveness will continue to be a demand of governments, private donors, and citizens. With increasing scrutiny of the uses of public and private monies allotted for charity or development projects, leaders should consider how their 5Ps can help them to practice effectiveness. It's not only showing the results now but getting better results using greater innovation and creativity, to maximize the use of resources.

Some of the larger trends shaping discourses and good practices in effectiveness are the following.

Triple Nexus. The convergence of development, humanitarian, and peacebuilding sectors—referred to as the Triple Nexus—means that there will be complementary, pooled, and interconnected programming, funding, and accountability, all created to harmonize efforts on the ground. We can no longer take a piecemeal approach. Things happen all at once, with enormous implications for current and future generations' security, survival, and well-being. A project in Bangladesh provides cooking gas to a refugee camp while planting trees to replace firewood in the surrounding area. A $100-million fund provides social services and work opportunities in areas destabilized by Boko Haram in West Africa, with multi-year grants allowing a project to change direction, if, for example, a drought sabotages an agriculture program.[1]

Creative Approaches. Fragility, conflict, and climate-induced crises in unstable contexts require creative approaches. On the ground, calls for innovative intervention are pivotal. Traditional actors must contend with new, non-traditional players from the private sector, as well as individual philanthropists, foundations, and diaspora organizations with more direct, timely, and less bureaucratic approaches. All must work collaboratively to secure long-term, multifaceted, holistic approaches to problems that a single, magic-bullet tactic or a past, flavor-of-the-month approach could not solve.

Localization and the Rise of New Responders. Local actors are the best at tackling new crises that emerge. They can take preventive action, seek the authorities' attention for a quick remedy, and provide active vigilance to preempt these crises from turning into large-scale disasters. As outlined in Principle 2, localization is at the heart of effective partnerships. Still, power, funding, and control have yet to trickle down to the brave workers in the trenches. Principle 10 discusses how those in the margins can, through localization and direct action, deploy innovation to achieve prosperity, growth, and economic development.

Adaptive Evaluation. Evaluating requires diverse, adaptive approaches, and critical perspectives that move away from donors' policy interests and agendas to a user-centric and complexity-based long view. Regional experts must be trained and professionalized to get this right. Having them trained will engender a shift from validation-seeking processes to ownership-driven processes where people can have the chance to sustain these changes. The wide sector involving practitioners and policymakers can benefit from more creative approaches to evaluating results.

Effectiveness Is the Daughter of Integrity

All the people I interviewed for this book are impact leaders in their own right. None expected a quick windfall from their initiatives. With limited time and financial resources to execute a project, they focused on the foundational aspects rather than on making assumptions too soon. They played the long game. They spent their time testing the partner, the design, the implementation, the capacity, and the alignment.

What does effectiveness mean? It runs the gamut of all development efforts and is especially critical for those who don't have larger organizational systems and processes, and who rely on a smaller set of parameters. Effectiveness means asking, "Have you accomplished what you set out to do?" Measure the impact of your interventions on a continued, sustainable basis. Principle 7 discusses the mechanics of your impact story and how you account for your results. As outlined in Principle 4, effectiveness also means being honest enough to recognize and potentially accept the unintended, unanticipated, and negative consequences of your actions.

The communities behind the success of the Community-Led Sanitation program in seven villages in Kwale country, Kenya, ended open defecation for good. Ten community leaders set themselves up as partners, not leaders, to address open defecation in communities through a participatory monitoring system. Once villagers had been educated, they decided to 'not eat their own shit'[2] and became advocates in other villages. Looking back, the volunteer monitoring committee reflected that they had to lead from behind and adjust their approach to trigger the right emotional commitment to the issue.

Your internal effectiveness should affect your external influence, leading to greater outcomes such as policy or program change, institutional supports, improved service delivery, or increased social awareness and healthy behaviors among partner communities. Risa Gold, the Executive Director of Miracle of Help (MoH), worked hard to build a strong relationship with the government to get the integrated community-development program in east Sierra Leone to become sustainable.[3] Aside from a focus on physical health, social health, and economic stability, they strengthened the government interface, building an office where local leaders could hold regular meetings with parliamentarians and elected community officers, so officials from UNICEF, Doctors without Borders, and other actors could ensure the community's voice was part of important decisions.

Four Strategies to Embed Effectiveness

A culture of effectiveness comes through in your everyday work. It's a mindset, a consistent practice, and a development principle to live by, that goes beyond books or reports. Practicing leadership is all about making effective decisions now.

1. *Build capacity.* Increase your change partner's capacity to determine outcomes in the short and long term. Invest in training, education, and the right software for data and strategic-knowledge management. The right amount of data with the right tools and mindset leads to greater effectiveness in the long run.

2. *Partner for results.* Partner with the people to increase the viability of any collection, measurement, and analysis of results—and to expand the ownership of these results. It is easy to design things from the top. The experience and satisfaction that come with co-designing together

are more important than outstanding reports put on shelves. It's not the output but the process that counts.

3. *Get useful feedback.* Avoid groupthink and other in-group bias when asking for feedback from change partners. Instead of asking point-blank if you have been effective, ask what needs changing or removing. Expect to be challenged. Don't settle for niceties.

4. *Don't overdo it.* Let go of the tendency to overdeliver and outperform. When you do more than you can, you push things off balance, creating pockets of high value and leaving the rest mediocre. You may also generate perverse results from overconcentration in some areas.

Unintended Benefits, Unexpected Drawbacks, and Perverse Consequences

According to the law of unintended consequences, there are always outcomes of deliberate actions that can't be foreseen. While this concept has been used to criticize government policies and programs in the United States, it applies broadly.

Don't worry about negative consequences. You'll know them when you see them. The real problem is the amount of time it can take for unintended and unanticipated results to surface, making any initiative vulnerable to a prolonged state of suspended judgment. Community improvement seldom shows its true colors in the earliest phases. This is incredibly frustrating for programmers and implementers eager to mitigate any unexpected results as soon as they emerge.

Advances in data science, probabilistic predictions, evaluation, measurement, and strategic risk management in private and public organizations have increased our potential to prevent and mitigate risk. We can apply our insights and understanding within the limits of these tools. Watching out for early-stage signs can give vital clues to what might be an unintended benefit, unexpected drawback, or perverse impact at its onset.

Unintended Benefits

We'd like to believe that more positive benefits accrue because of our actions on the ground. While the Theory of Change mentioned in Principle 2 does not identify unintended benefits, these can move the needle on your issue area as well, and be a welcome development. But what to do with them? It's an important consideration given that anything unintended requires some action or inaction on your part. A decision to act on these benefits might lead to scope creep and loss of focus on critical targets.

Some examples of unintended benefits include:

- The demilitarized zones on the Korean Peninsula that have led to the flourishing of natural habitats.
- A school-building project that became a hub for mothers to sit and discuss their problems while waiting for their children. Soon, the school built a water supply so mothers could get their jars filled, and it attracted community-based programs on health, nutrition, and safety.

Unexpected Drawbacks

Unexpected drawbacks are negative consequences or ambiguous impacts that affect your projects and require you to change your tactics midway. You can't predict the extent to which these drawbacks could harm your project's success. Sometimes, they impel you to create a new project, with its own tactics.

Some examples of unexpected drawbacks:

- In the eastern villages of Ghana in 2013, nets meant for mosquitos were instead used by farmers as fishing nets or curtains.
- A Ministry of Education withdraws regular budgetary support from a school, after hearing of an external donor's strong community leadership and financial

backing of the building and facilities. Though the new school is an excellent addition to the Ministry, the annual budgeting cycle has left it financially unsupported for an entire year. Teachers make up extended teaching time without additional pay.

Perverse Consequences

Perverse consequences are negative or aberrant effects that do the opposite of what you wanted to achieve. Implemented solutions to a policy or program end up in practices and behaviors that game the system and produce more harmful effects. Wrong stimulation in politics and business can cause such perverse consequences, and it's the same with development.

Some examples of perverse consequences:

- During the British India days, the cobra policy stated that the catcher would get a bounty for every cobra caught. This policy became so successful that citizens were breeding cobras so that they could get more income. When the British found out, they dismantled the incentive, and the breeders let loose all the cobras, the effect being more cobras than ever. This became known as the Cobra Effect.

- A school attracts more enrolments every year to the detriment of underpaid teachers. Overwhelmed with demand, the school principal implements a fundraising project to compensate for teachers' pay and maintain the school's overall upkeep. The fundraiser keeps the teachers' attention divided and leads to a mediocre education for students.

- A neighborhood notices a private donor has built a new school in another neighborhood and asks the donor to see their own neighborhood and propose a school for their children. Soon, more petitions for schools arise that the private donor can't handle, and the donor leaves the community for good.

Timing Is about Trial and Error

Getting results could take a lifetime of work, or could involve an exact, targeted few months or years. Timing entails building trust, and synergy. Some things to think about:

1. *Imperfection.* Your actions will seldom be perfect the first time. Allow yourself and the community sharing your vision room to grow and adapt.
2. *Capacity building.* Assuming all actors are on board, invest in capacity-building all the time, every time. It's always the people, not the building, the roads, the bridge, the clinics. Appropriate use and management of these resources requires strong leaders and engaged followers.
3. *Know them enough.* You will always feel like an outsider who doesn't know enough for others to trust you. Take small steps. Don't rush to decide or make judgments. Avoid artificial timelines. Know all the interests at play: personal, organizational, group. Seize the opportunity to safeguard these interests.
4. *Test yourself.* Principle 2 discusses zeroing in on you and your change partner's value. Do you have selection criteria for selecting a partner, setting the right project, harnessing local processes, and learning and improving?
5. *Make it straightforward.* Choose approaches that will enable you to fast-track your results without having to make unnecessary reiterations.
6. *Test the change partner:*
(a) For understanding. Do they understand the role they will play now, and in the future, once you partner

with them? Are expectations clear and well-articulated, formally and informally?

(b) For resolve. Do they have the determination to overcome foreseen and unforeseen impediments that are bound to come their way? Are they prepared to use existing assets and apply creativity to solve problems?

(c) For commitment. Are they prepared for the task at hand? Are they willing to co-share the costs and the ultimate responsibility of stewardship and leadership?

Big Data Is Not the Answer

We use technology to help us get better at asking the right questions. I hear about Big Data all the time, but Big Data hasn't arrived yet for the developing world. Even as they call blockchain the next game-changer, it has yet to create significant ripples in Africa and developing Asia.[4] Forget blockchain or Big Data. Let's talk Internet: access to broadband in the world's poorest countries lags behind the world's median average.

Big Data, a term coined in 1997 by NASA scientists Michael Cox and David Ellsworth, is the vast amount of data generated by supercomputers.[5] Currently, Big Data comes from but is not limited to data from social media, SMS-based communication, satellite feeds, media, and other digital information. It may be structured or unstructured with three characteristics: volume, variety, and velocity.[6]

Rescue operations during Typhoon Haiyan in 2014 used Big Data extensively, as was previously done with the Haiti Earthquake and Pakistan Floods. Rescuers used mobile-phone data to track accurate locations for rescue operations and personnel deployment and infrastructure on the ground. Massive amounts of data from social media sites, tweets, and calls for help mapped out where rescuers needed to go first.[7] Big Data saved thousands of lives, and continues to. For example, Big Data helped medical researchers aggregate cancer data from patients and their tumors that will enable clinicians to detect cancer earlier, or find new treatments. It helped reduce fatalities in road accidents in Edmonton by aggregating data from traffic cameras, roadside sensors, and roadside devices to identify high-risk locations and make structural-engineering improvements.

Data is never neutral. It is bound by context, creation, and use. Data is mediated in socio-political realms, making it a live construct. Recent academic research on the uses of crowdsourced Big Data that aided responses to the Haiti Earthquake and Nepal Earthquake showed the data underwent several mutations as it was collected. Indeed, information processing and interpretation tended to exclude communities that had contributed the data to begin with, making these communities marginal to the decision-making affecting their lives.[8]

Digital inequality, lack of access to translated knowledge, lack of Information and Communications Technology (ICT) infrastructures, and the identity markers of caste, gender, ethnicity, and literacy, are conditions that hinder full citizen participation in the promise of Big Data. Ethics remain a serious concern. There are no controls for the massive amounts of information about public citizens collected for use.

Consider *thick data*, rather than Big Data. We need thick data to analyze the social meanings behind the numbers. Thick data are about understanding social phenomena, which require thick descriptions. Clifford Geertz described how thick descriptions of human behavior include detailed data collection and analysis of the context in which behavior occurs. In short, it's about the qualitative nature of the data, which contains insights, motivations, preferences, aspirations— telling us *"how and why people do what they do."*[9] Principle 7 discusses how stories can be a powerful vehicle for articulating your interesting vision for the future.

For example, the city of Rockford, Illinois, achieved functional-zero chronic homelessness in 2017 because of the innovative ways in which it collected data on the unhoused population. The city rewired the concept of "Housing First," centering basic needs for the unhoused rather than, for example, job applications or substance-abuse treatment. They collaborated with different providers differently. The shift in data came about when they used Point-in-Time, a real-time census of all the unhoused in Rockford listed by name in Google Docs. With names of actual people, city programmers saw people, not numbers to be controlled. The data became real for them.[10]

Rapid changes in the environment, the multifaceted needs of communities, and the variability of consequences require a long-game-effectiveness focus. Asking the right questions is superior to generating data through statistics, studies, or experiments. Deriving meaning from data is an irreplaceable human function for sense-making.

Summary:
Reflective Questions Using the Global Impact Leadership Framework

In the space below, reflect on how to play the effectiveness long-game using the 5Ps: Purpose, Passion, Provision, Practice, and Paradigm.

- How can global impact leaders respond to and implement the four significant trends listed above (triple nexus, creative approaches, localization, and adaptive evaluation)?

- Reflect on the unintended, unanticipated and perverse consequences of your own work. What have you learned?

- How can you embed effectiveness at your organization or within your development plan?

Principle 4

Learn from Mistakes

The fourth principle for global impact leaders is to learn from your mistakes and the mistakes of others. Failures are essential reminders of the need to improve. Not bothering to stop and scrutinize your mistakes is fatal. Define your success and decide how far you're willing to go to accomplish your personal and organizational objectives. Most of the time, breakthroughs in the form of mistakes guide the best actions. To engage with failure is to be human.

Eric Rajah, co-founder of A Better World (ABW), believes in training local leaders to be responsible for their change efforts. He recalled that, six months after the grand opening of a school ABW funded, students were not attending classes in the new building. It turned out the ground on which the school was built was sinking. The local school board managed the construction and had awarded the contract to a relative of the school-board director. Eric told the school board the ABW would not work with them again unless they fixed the problem. The school board asked their Member of Parliament (MP) to intercede with ABW on their behalf but received censure from the MP.[1]

The experience was a lesson learned. After the incident, any ABW community project requires an assessment of capacity, and working with community members on the design, management, monitoring, and evaluation of projects. To grasp the context, ABW listens to the people, tries to understand their concerns and needs, and estimates their capacities and existing assets.

ABW decided not to work in one community in a particular country. "The community leaders asked for things they don't need," says Rajah. In the case of the faulty school building, certain community members were more interested in money than in improving the quality of life for those around them.

Three Types of Failure

The failure industry is booming. New leadership science encourages leaders to fail forward, fail fast, and fail good. There is now a failure museum, failure roundtables, and, of course, water-cooler talks about who's failing most constructively. Organizations are launching failure conversations to learn within their sectors.

There's nothing wrong with all of this, unless failure discourse takes over—at the expense of concrete corrections. Inside and outside organizations, failure should not be limited to reflection. Learning from failures is, however, easier said than done. Many reviews, evaluations, assessments, and postmortem talks stop at probing what went wrong. Leaders must create a safe space where their people can speak up about what's not working well, get heads together to solve problems or even small troubles, and encourage bad or even troublesome reporting. Provocateurs like you can set the foundation for learning in your organization or networks, without repercussions to your jobs or reputations.

There are good and bad failures. You must distinguish between the two and apply the right context. Failures because of deviations from the norm, operating standards, and processes are preventable, and should not be repeated. But intelligent failures, which happen in innovation mode, should be encouraged. Everyone, including individual agents and multilateral organizations, makes mistakes in the laboratory we call social development.

Action failures are committed by individuals and groups as they work on projects and initiatives that generate unintended consequences. Every impact leader will make mistakes as part of their learning curve, without serious fallout to their change partners or themselves. As a provocateur, you will be blamed for almost everything but seldom credited for the success. Get used to it.

Institutional failures are policy failures based on errors of judgment, such as the 2008 financial crisis and the decades-long attempt to lift Africa from poverty through global aid. The latter is an example of adhering to the so-called rules of the game despite evidence to the contrary. The former involves systemic complicity, a widespread culture of greed, and lack of accountability from financial institutions and their accomplices.

By 2008 the culture of greed and impunity among those in power had to be dealt with legally and culturally. Despite the massive protests of the Occupy Movement, only a few executives were convicted for illegal actions. Many perpetrators got away with a slap on the hand, and there were extensive government bailouts in the billions. Larger bureaucratic structures rarely reward reflexive processes until the problem has become too complex or large to rein in.

Recent literature on HIV/AIDS and development work notes the importance of African perspectives, especially citizens and village leaders who mediate between global policies and their own needs. The HIV/AIDS responses did not consider the role of traditional leaders and wide disconnection between the international donors and the local people; the latter viewed HIV/AIDS as not a social good for all.

Ethical failures are those that occur when individuals are administratively and even criminally culpable for violating the rules of engagement. They can include, for instance, allegations of sexual harassment, or of persecuting whistleblowers. Unfortunately, rape, sex trafficking, and prostitution within the humanitarian sector are rife. Abuse of power, the cowboy mentality, lack of accountability, and impunity continue to erode humanitarian workers' and the public's trust in the industry, and are leading to sweeping reforms.[2]

Two recent, high-profile ethical failures come to mind: Greg Mortenson of Central Asia Institute (CAI), famous for his book *Three Cups of Tea* (and already mentioned in Principle 1), and Marc and Craig Kielburger, of the WE Charity, formerly Free the Children. Mortenson was accused of manipulation, distortion, and exaggeration, including providing misinformation on the number of schools CAI built, among other things. The Kielburgers faced conflict-of-interest allegations after Canadian Prime Minister Justin Trudeau and the Federal Liberals awarded WE $900 million to implement a federal grant program to mobilize student volunteers during the COVID-19 crisis.

Mortenson, like many humanitarians, started with good intentions. But he didn't value honesty, integrity, and accuracy; the public subsequently turned away from him and devalued his contributions to Afghan communities. The WE Charity controversy provided much-needed soul-searching for the Canadian development sector, which could have grounded WE's understanding of rights, equity, and sustainability in development.

When Success Is an Obstacle to a Breakthrough

Obsessed with success, individuals and organizations cannot stop, look at, and listen to what is actually going on. Maybe they haven't been present for decades in the communities they claim to serve. Fixed agendas that are overly prescriptive and lacking in intuition will never work. Homegrown inventions and innovations are ripe for the picking. Identifying and honing what works already doesn't have to be rocket science.

Success for success's sake is useless. We know success can lead to personal ruin, but an organization must be equally conscious of its downsides. Achievement provides a feeling of invincibility, of "having arrived," but it leads to complacency and stagnation.

Critics disapproved of the highly successful global campaigns to fight TB, HIV/AIDS, malaria, and others, because they emphasized the importance of support for large-scale holistic investments in healthcare infrastructures in developing countries. For generations, lack of adequate financing and well-trained health personnel, as well as dated bureaucratic structures, prevented these health systems from focusing on patient-centered healthcare.[3]

Success through the growth mindset can impede learning. Recently, I have seen a glut of meta-information: evaluations of evaluations, assessments of assessments, reports of reports. These can represent the perfection of the craft of evaluation, assessments, reporting—of building evidence, horizontal and vertical alignments, integrations, and systems harmonization. However, this overemphasis on good housekeeping, informed by the need for efficiencies because of austerity, should translate to lasting changes in interventions. It rarely does.

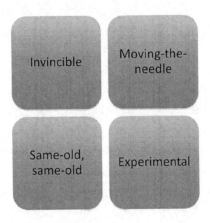

Figure 5: Success Versus Breakthrough

Figure 5 showcases the relationship between success and breakthroughs with the 5Ps.

An organization or individual *low on success and breakthroughs* repeats the same old business approach. The NGO business model, for instance, is ready for total overhaul: it is never about outcomes and execution speed, the two most prized qualities in our hyper-networked society.

An organization or individual *high on success and low on breakthroughs* thinks they are invincible but seldom makes waves. There's plenty of evidence that structural policy adjustments in the past did not lift millions from poverty in nations that borrowed from the World Bank and IMF. They measured success in growth in investments, balance of payments, privatization of public services, which favored the ruling elites in developing countries. Recent studies surfaced the elite capture of aid which confirms the long-standing hypothesis that aid corruption existed.[4]

An organization or individual *high on breakthroughs and low on success* sells experimental methods rather than the outcomes derived from them. There are plenty of laboratories, prizes, and innovation challenges that favor breakthroughs, which may or may not be viable when reality hits. Funded by "failure money," these experiments are high on optimism and confirmation bias, which can easily lead to false positives.

With *an equal amount of success and breakthroughs*, provocateurs can move the needle on the most seemingly intractable social ills of our time. With the Global Impact Leadership Framework, the whole is more than the sum of its parts. You, the provocateur, move forward by balancing success with breakthroughs on the ground.

Success is a byproduct of passion, purpose, provision, practice, and the correct paradigm(s). Practice is the determiner here. You are not obsessed and consumed with success. You facilitate it, but do not place undue onus on it, within what your partnership reasonably demands. When success is inevitable, it reflects the community's effort. It is not a function of your popularity or the convenience of your presence and direction.

Success could look like the shape of an impact on partners' lives, as well as their changed outlook. These kinds of successes are hard to measure, but should be apparent enough for an outsider to confirm. In Principle 8, on living the legacy, I touch on what objectives would create a sense of accomplishment for you.

The Writing's Already on the Wall

In Principle 3, I defined and discussed unintended, unanticipated, and negative consequences of development-oriented actions. Twenty-twenty hindsight could be two to three years down the road and, before that, there may be fallout which you did not expect or prepare for. You can, however, anticipate that there will be some kind of failing in various parts of your intervention. If you're doing deep work, not cosmetic retouching, expect obstacles.

Learning from the mistakes and experiences of others is underrated. The use of case studies, role play, and direct observations in classrooms all over the world points to its effectiveness. In the entrepreneurial ecosystem, failure is already publicly celebrated. In the development sector, managers must reward bad reports and normalize this habit, period.

For example, TechnoServe[5] hosted its first failure conference in 2013, sharing six failures and what they learned. Among them was a grant that encouraged entrepreneurs to build growth businesses in Mpumalanga, South Africa. The goal, based on a successful project in another province, was to find 20 businesses to employ 150 people each. The project failed. The Water, Sanitation, Hygiene (WASH) sector in Africa is marked by many horrific failures and is only beginning to see the benefits of shared analysis, which leads to improved actions and preventative work on the ground.[6]

Learning doesn't take place in isolation. Your change partner and your support networks should be excellent sounding boards for your projects. They can help you identify areas you might have overlooked or issues that can arise because of blind spots. Seek opinions from your best critics or even from less supportive colleagues. In fact, if you want to learn from others' mistakes, detach yourself from your agenda, politics, and recipes. A provocateur I interviewed for this book noted that she received some harsh comments that her "pie-in-the-sky" project ideas are impossible to execute. This didn't deter her, but she took the comments as a warning to be brutally realistic and avoid tunnel vision. It's up to you to find the gems in the criticisms.

Another way to learn from others is to cultivate role models who are precisely what you're not. Surround yourself, not just with people, but ideas, thought patterns, and alternative explanations that you will never encounter unless you seek them out. Because most of you are not working in formal organizational structures, develop a personal Board of Directors, without them knowing about it. Make use of these informal advisors, people you can call for contrarian perspectives, and with whom you can permit yourself to be vulnerable.

Ask the actual experts such as those who have survived giant typhoons, evacuated thousands of residents, created livelihoods, and supported their recovery. Ask the people in the slum communities how they flourish every day. Ask those in refugee camps how to create social businesses that thrive. Ask those who survive droughts every year how they not just cope but become resilient within their habitats. They hold unique insights seldom captured in academic journals and policy briefs. Seek mentorship with real-world experts.

Be comfortable with vulnerability. Donors want to showcase success and pick the easiest, most well-traveled roads, to avoid incurring overwhelming risk. Donor-facing development incentivizes the copy/paste approach. Within your sphere of influence, create conditions that reward candor and open conversations for eliminating the stigma of making mistakes. Talk about failures the way you talk about successes. Use stories to encourage others, seek out alternatives, and not give up. You'll choose better partners, raise more funds, and determine metrics without having to suffer pointlessly.

Five Strategies to Celebrate Failure
without the Drama

Within the contemporary media context, public confessions become spectacles. Truthfulness and sincere apologies for wrongdoings that hurt people and communities are a rarity. As we become numb to confessionals and the theatricality of vulnerability, it is clear that any drama attached to failure has simply become a waste of energy.

We can build a culture of truthfulness that frees people from naming and shaming tactics, including their current iteration: cancel culture. We should expect that our leaders be fallible, but assume they can discern and make correct decisions most of the time. With practice, we can commit to learning from our own and others' failures with efficacy. Here are five ways to reframe failures as a provocateur:

1. *Accept failure without defensiveness.* As much as you desire success and achievement, accept failure as a fact of life. There is no winning without trying. Failure means you are trying, and still trying.

2. *Engage with failure.* What happened here? Objectively assess, and include others in the analysis. Find the root cause and eliminate it, if possible. Honestly sharing your failures and mistakes opens doors to authentic conversations with others who have done the same, or would like to know. Being vulnerable is a sign of grit, not weakness.

3. *Act quickly.* Instead of harping on about the past, handle setbacks immediately and correct mistakes right away. Acting decisively will encourage you to focus on quick wins.

4. *Build stamina* for mid- and long-term horizons, so failures don't sting as much. Set your standards high so when you bounce back, you do it stronger, and your

benchmarks grow with you.

5. *Keep a positive growth mindset.* Be patient with yourself and with your change partner. Defining failures and successes with them and showing how they can learn from both is the most important thing. Leverage your failures for breakthroughs.

If failure is the new success, are you accepting yours with style and grace? As a global impact leader, your mistakes are more than meets the eye. Indeed, it's what happens in your head and the remedial actions you take that matter. It's your and your change partner's jobs to define, measure, and own your actions. With your eyes on the prize, breakthroughs will become more important than successes, by far.

Summary:
Reflective Questions Using the Global Impact Leadership Framework

In the space below, reflect on the questions using the 5Ps— Purpose, Passion, Provision, Practice, and Paradigm. Remember, you can use the 5Ps to reframe the concept of failure.

• What could success look like from your perspective, and what does failure mean?

• When have you learned the most from your mistakes and failures? Whom do you admire from having learned from their failures?

• What challenges do you see in learning and growing through failures in the sector or broader community where you belong?

Principle 5

Access Your Ignorance and Borrow Shamelessly

The fifth principle for global impact leaders is to be honest about your ignorance, and then to borrow well. Quick fixes, cyclical responses, and prefabricated interventions do not encourage lasting change on the ground. As I've demonstrated in previous Principles, terrible mistakes can happen using this approach without proper anchors. Best practices are already alive and well in many communities and organizations. As a global impact leader, you'll need to be able to access your ignorance, embrace it, and learn to cultivate homegrown ideas to facilitate change.

Cidalia Luis-Akbar said: "You can help those you don't know and don't need to agree with. You don't even need to understand. With little money, you can make a big difference. You can build a school in a village that will never have the opportunity to have schools."[1] A businesswoman based in Washington, DC, she helped turn an orphanage in Bamyan, Afghanistan, into a school in 2008. She knew the lasting benefits of investing in boys and girls. With the Ayenda Foundation, she worked with the Ambassador of Afghanistan and his wife, as well as other leaders, through many fundraising dinners. Former Prime Minister Hamid Karzai donated the land for the school and paid the teachers' salaries.

A native of Portugal, Cidalia had no firsthand knowledge of Afghanistan except through her husband, Muhammad. They had wanted to adopt an Afghan child but couldn't because of the country's policy. Having been childless for years, the couple channeled that desire into helping Afghan children have a strong chance for a better life.

At first, they conceived of a day school in Bamyan for Hazara girls and boys orphaned from the 2001 bombing. After the bombing, the orphans lived in caves. The Taliban hated this place because of the powerful women leaders who lived there, and the Buddha statues. Cidalia and the community leaders later decided a school would provide the best protection and care for the children.

She didn't stop helping even though she didn't know much about the country and the magnitude of the issues involved to begin with. But when she visited for the first time, she was exposed to the plight of the children as opposed to the lavish lifestyles of the elites of the country. She embraced her ignorance and learned firsthand from those who had the know-how and the cultural intelligence on how the school could be built and sustained.

The Benefits of Accessing Your Ignorance

Ignorance can be your best friend. As outlined in Principle 4, when presented with unknowns and ambiguous situations in which mistakes are made, the provocateur leans on their ignorance and asks probing questions. Your change partners will appreciate your attempt to understand them and their position, and not preempt their needs with a formula for success.

Ignorance isn't usually seen as a good thing. Technically, however, ignorance simply means you do not know. In the context of development, it also means you are not beholden to a prefabricated solution, method, or approach. A customized approach, informed by how you acknowledge your ignorance, trumps the assumed brilliance of "the one way."

Embracing your ignorance frees you from being perceived as, and from acting as, an all-knowing expert. It frees both partners from unrealistic expectations at the outset. You are a catalyst, not a source. Your relationship with the change partner becomes a joint exploration and future-facing project. Embracing your ignorance equalizes potential imbalances and empowers all involved to give more than they get. Every process becomes part of the intervention.

As a provocateur aligned with the Global Impact Leadership Framework, you are mindful of your prejudices and limits. Information is not the problem. Information inundates us daily, but not the wisdom and distilled insights of practice. Addressing your positionality and asking questions about differences are the beginning of wisdom.

Most times, as a practitioner in global development working with the marginalized, I found it was better to ask great questions than to provide brilliant answers. I worked with a regional social-enterprise organization for three years back in the late 2000s. I led an e-commerce training program where participants learned how to market and trade through the Internet with their buyers. E-commerce, if done right, yields more economic returns—at least 120%—compared with traditional selling. In 2008, this was relatively novel in developing Asian economies. As I worked on my project, it gradually became clear why there was lack of e-commerce training interest and poor subsequent uptake among artisans and small producers: Internet access was uneven and expensive. Looking back, we should have analyzed externalities, such as technological, economic, and environmental contexts, and internal management capacity and technical competency, before embarking on such a costly venture.

In practical terms, accessing your ignorance means:

- *Do your homework diligently.* Test assumptions and unearth underlying issues like an investigative journalist. Collect diverse ideas and viewpoints that do not sit well with your hypothesis.
- *Don't do it all yourself.* When presented with issues beyond your capacity or ability to comprehend, bring these to your change partners instead of figuring it all out yourself. They own the problem, and they should

own the solution. Avoid self-limiting scripts in your head about yourself and your partner's capacity.

- *Validate* but move forward. As a provocateur, you don't need someone to greenlight your projects when there's evidence of proof of concept. Ignorance doesn't mean being uncertain and tentative.

- *Wait for the cues in your interactions.* Don't jump to conclusions and try to reconcile complex issues for the sake of appeasement. You need to know the backstory. Most people will gladly reveal the underlying tensions and past histories between individuals and groups that will inform how the project will unfold.

The Temptation to Join the Quick Wins

Anything that gets traction in development involves money. Follow the money trail, and you will see hundreds of actors, each in their tiny spaces of action, representing their organization's interests, agendas, and products.

In 2013, Typhoon Haiyan hit the western islands of Samar and Leyte in the Philippines hard. According to the UN, at least 6,300 died and 11 million were affected by the disaster.[2] Hundreds of relief operators descended, set up shop, and provided immediate relief to thousands of affected people. Large multinationals came with cars, jeeps, mobile hospitals, ships, air cargo, global staff, and other massive infrastructure. The national government's actions and those of the local community were incapable of credible and efficient response at the early stages. Celebrities came and went, bringing immediate supplies, cash donations, and media attention. There were also predatory and unscrupulous groups with dubious, non-humanitarian interests. Many wanted to help but ended up making a mess.

The number of players was staggering. There were NGO coordination committees for Water & Sanitation, Health,

Education, Nutrition, Child Protection, and Cash Transfer at the local, provincial, national, regional, and international levels. Five levels of action by at least 15 to 20 humanitarian groups were at play, including the major UN agencies, foreign governments' disaster responses, interregional and country-level representatives of embassies, and consulate offices, not to mention the local clubs and charities.

Three months after the disaster, during my reconnaissance in the area, I saw new actors encamped in various parts of the city and the outlying regions, notably from Taiwan, other smaller NGOs, and charity and Filipino-diaspora groups. Seven years after the disaster, reports surfaced of corruption, red tape, and mismanagement that bogged down reconstruction. Thousands of disaster survivors continue to live in makeshift shelters, waiting for help to transition into better housing and income opportunities.[3]

There are massive amounts of duplication, overlap, and uneven results in this scenario. Scope creep can also surface, among other management issues. When many actors converge, coordination is often limited to information-sharing and rarely gets more substantive. Community partners on the ground who will live with the aftermath get the short end of the stick.

It's effortless to get money and support right away for relief and recovery in a disaster situation like this. But when the media's gone and the buzz dies down, the long-term, painful task of rebuilding gets orphaned.

Development is where the rubber hits the road. It's not fancy, heroic, and glamorous, but a commitment to work for a long-term goal. Every community has a history and a future. Take the time to know their experiences with charitable individuals and groups, the projects they conducted, their successes, and their lessons learned.

Brilliant Ideas Come from Places You'd Least Expect

There are a million ideas for global solutions to complex problems. There has been a proliferation of innovation labs in development, and they have confirmed that experimenting with solutions saves time and costs, and designing for users with closed feedback loops helps social-good agents, the private sector, and governments.

However, we don't need labs to tell us how to think, imagine, and be successful.

Laboratories and experiments are cocooned environments where failures are encouraged, not punished. You can conduct as many trials as you want without defaulting on your mortgage payments. There is always a supply of prestigious funding and support for bright, ambitious, and driven minds to make use of. Outside the labs, however, storms are brewing, and placebos aren't relevant. The helping industry is a contact sport. Principle 4 elucidates this important insight.

In 2015, I was part of a prestigious fellowship program that housed us for three months. We had free board, stipends, and local and international field trips to open our minds with new insights. With 90% of us already successful in our jobs, careers, and projects, the experience felt limited; I believe we had more to give to the world than sitting and listening to lectures by known luminaries, researchers, and academics. Imagine what we could have accomplished in three months of fieldwork. The best instruction is out there, and it involves implementing initiatives and returning with concrete learning, including feedback.

Here are some of the samples of African and Asian innovations drastically transforming their respective continents—homegrown solutions that defy orthodox approaches:[4]

- A strain of sweet potato cures blindness in children that is caused by Vitamin A deficiency.

- A strong oral tradition in Uganda helps child combatants deal with the traumas of war.
- Aid supplies are produced in Africa for use in the region, prepositioning supplies and materials for rescue, relief, and rehabilitation.
- Refining locally sourced cassava into ethanol fuel provides cleaner cooking fuel to replace wood and charcoal, which cause deforestation and respiratory problems.
- In the lowlands of Bangladesh, farmers turn to a centuries-old form of hydroponics to create floating vegetable gardens. The UN Food and Agricultural Organization declare Bangladesh's floating gardens to be a globally important agricultural heritage site in December 2015.[5]
- Larvae from black soldier flies eat food waste from 200 restaurants in China.[6]
- In May 2016, the Government of Rwanda starts using drones to deliver all blood products for 20 hospitals and health centers, improving access to healthcare for millions of Rwandans.[7]

Jerry Sternin, a former Save the Children employee, once said, "The traditional model for social and organizational change doesn't work. It never has. You can't bring permanent solutions in from outside. Instead, find small, successful, but 'deviant' practices already working in the organization and amplify them. Maybe the answer is already alive in the organization—and change comes when you find it."[8]

Sternin and his wife addressed the malnutrition issue in Vietnam's local villages within six months by figuring out who was successful and healthier than others with the same resources. The mothers in these villages were collecting tiny shrimps and crabs in nearby paddies every day and, along with sweet-potato greens, adding them to their children's diets. The mothers were also feeding their children three to four times a day as opposed to the customary two meals.

The couple amplified what they were doing and shared these practices with the rest of the villagers. Within two years, malnutrition was eradicated. Call it the positive-deviant theory: in every community, organization, or social group, there are individuals whose exceptional behaviors or practices get better results than their neighbors with the same resources. Without realizing it, these positive deviants have discovered the path to success for the entire group—as long as their secrets can be analyzed, isolated, and shared.

Where can we find ideas to leverage change? Where do we look? Expand your mind and find that treasure from underresourced but inspiration-rich areas.

- *Look* at things in the interstices of various disciplines and fields. Somewhere in these spaces, things are ripe for the picking.
- *Extrapolate* what exists and works in the natural world and use the same ideas for human coexistence and regeneration. Consider permaculture, a philosophy that provides design strategies ensuring entire ecosystems will be regenerative and self-sufficient.
- *Learn* from the failures of others. There are different definitions of success, prosperity, peace, and sufficiency. The rest can teach the West about many great things.

Borrow Shamelessly

Borrowing from other areas of human endeavor has long been proven to work. The rapid pace of technological change has enabled organizations to become more explorative in their borrowing efforts. Borrowing demonstrates interest, capacity, and commitment to experimenting with what works in the field. Much of what exists in management and leadership in the development sector originated from the business world. Performance-management tools, knowledge management, recruitment practices, including procurement mechanisms, are applied widely in the sector. Implementation science is influenced by many interdisciplinary advances.

Today, the latest discoveries in design, neuroscience, and data unlock insights into individual and organizational behaviors. Development requires a behavioral change in various actors that will lead to broader social-good outcomes. When "new" insights are uncovered—for example how children learn in refugee settings, or how the rural poor benefit from a cash-transfer program—these complement the experiential, participatory, people-centered expertise that already lies in many change contexts.

Let's look at the lean approach. Instead of focusing on problems and needs, lean thinking focuses on solutions, considering the experiences of end-users of solution-based interventions. Rapid feedback from users engenders a series of tests that find the most optimal products and services for targeted users. Instead of traditional monitoring and evaluation, the feedback-to-market approach validates and tests assumptions immediately, with fewer costs and less time.

Six Things to Consider When Using a Borrowed Idea

Check the origins, benefits, and context of an idea. Borrowing hook, line, and sinker rarely works. It's amateurish and irresponsible. Is there a local idea or concept you can use instead of something from elsewhere? In the Philippines, we have the concept of *bayanihan*: coming together as a community to acknowledge the deep cultural and historical roots of our national psyches. In the African region, *ubuntu* means "I am because we are," the close integration of personhood with greater humanity.

- *If you borrow a foreign concept, idea, or solution, do your research.* If your country is the poorest in Africa and your government wants to replicate the educational approaches of Denmark, your issue is comparability. Get an objective opinion on how it can be applied in your own change context.

- *How will change partners embrace the idea politically, socially, logically, and culturally?* Will there be a risk of adoption? Account for and adjust to these factors.

- Budget time and training costs. It takes time before an approach can be fully integrated into lives and communities. Find advocates and early adopters.

- *Who are the resistors and what are their reasons for resisting?* Look for underlying causes and needs. There will always be organizational, systemic, and personal needs underlying any objections.

- *Consistently reinforce newly learned behavior and thinking with incentives and practical application.*

As a provocateur, harness the exemplars in your midst who provide contrarian views on what works and why it works. Borrow shamelessly and give the people the credit they deserve when they offer a staggering amount of evidence that local solutions provide the finest option. A solutions-centered approach is better than a problem-focused intervention.

Summary:
Reflective Questions Using the Global
Impact Leadership Framework

In the space below, reflect on the questions using the 5Ps—Purpose, Passion, Provision, Practice, and Paradigm. Embracing your ignorance gives you vast potential because it rejects any pre-determined framework of action.

- When working with change partners, how can you benefit from suspending judgment and acknowledging your limits?

- How do you spot and nurture homegrown ideas into positive innovation?

- Which action areas call for borrowing creatively from other disciplines?

Principle 6

Don't Underestimate Your Impact

The sixth principle for global impact leaders is in the name: impact. You must have an unrelenting focus on and relationship to impact, which demands greater accountability and transparency, and attention to results in various collective and individual efforts. Your results mindset is the best antidote to overreach. Through your organization or your networks, you can take concrete steps to eradicate complacency and waste, and arrive at an impact you can be proud of. As a small actor, your norm should be relational accountability, based on higher levels of trust. Impact will always be non-negotiable.

What Results?

Everyone in the social-good sector knows they must be results oriented if they want to make a difference. Their performance should match organizational and program objectives. According to the *Canadian Oxford Dictionary*, the noun "accountability" is derived from the adjective "accountable," which means "responsible; required to account for one's conduct."

Accountability isn't solely for organizations or those who are part of a larger network. You may not have an affiliation at all, but your impact can still be results oriented. In fact, having no organizational affiliation could positively affect how you parse results. You can set the deliverables and the assessment strategies. You can choose the donors with whom you want to work and know the results they expect.

Being aware of this principle is just good sense. Not all activities are equal, not all partnerships are robust, and not all investments of staff or volunteer time and monies yield the same dividends on the ground. In this section, I understand results and outcomes synonymously. Outcomes are long-lasting, positive effects of interventions or activities conducted in communities and locations identified through an *a priori*—reason-based—process.

Over the last two decades, in social-good organizations, including the public sector, results orientation has become the norm rather than a "good to have." Results can come in a myriad of forms, from small activities conducted straightforwardly or interventions in complex systems and environments involving various actors and mandates with different interpretations of success and achievements.

The gold standard of results orientation is that interventions should contribute to sustainable, encompassing, positive change in the behavior and attitudes of people and communities. These changes will engender more profound transformations in societies based on their self-determination and agency. Decades of aid history show the education of women in many impoverished communities is one of the best strategies to lift a subset of the population out of poverty. Educated women are assets not only to their immediate families but also to their neighbors, communities, and networks. There is now solid evidence of the ripple effect of women's education in most developing countries.

Using light-learning outcome-based approaches, you can determine what changes have taken place with interventions at the household, communal/community, regional, and national levels, with fewer budgetary and time demands. Such approaches will allow you to find out which interventions produced the most promising and relevant outcomes. For example, outcome harvesting is used to "harvest" outcomes and work backwards to piece them together to determine which intervention made this happen and how it did so.

Principle 2 asks you to identify your value statement,

zero in on your change partner, and realize your Theory of Change. The Theory of Change is your impact story, more or less. Results orientation integrates the theory into the strategic core of the organization, making sure there are no one-off incidents in an organization busy doing outstanding work.

Whose Results Matter?

There is near total consensus among practitioners that the results achieved by the change partners matter the most. You, the global impact leader, should be clear on this from the very beginning. Yet, the abundance of market-based solutions to development problems skews results to those who initiate the change rather than those on the receiving end.

The CEO of a nonprofit organization training women leaders of social enterprises told me in an interview that they measure results not only in the traditional sense of improvement to beneficiaries, but also through donors' engagement. The CEO is accountable to those individual private donors who are giving their money to the worthy cause the organization represents. This shift in perspective is an unfortunate product of the "marketization of development,"[1] which stresses a business mindset, with mixed results.

Asking "Whose results matter?" means determining who will get the most significant benefit from your impact work. Who has the greatest need? There will be second-, third-, and fourth-tier benefits enjoyed by different stakeholders. Still, you should be explicit and unabashedly committed to those whose needs are most met by your work.

You can benefit substantially from a results-orientation framework that puts strategy, people, measurements, and resources together.

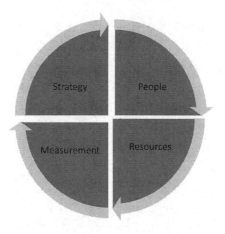

Figure 6: Results-Orientation Framework

1. *Strategy.* A clear, compelling, strategic motive separates a great results orientation from something dictated by outside parties, such as funders. Find the time and resources to bring all accountability demands under the overall organizational or corporate strategy. For example, a partnership with an organization based in Sierra Leone that only supplies books and sends out educational experts to train local teachers could simply look at immediate outcomes. Since this is the only mission, it seems to make strategic sense. A mere focus on projects and activities, however, can limit the utility and spread of benefits. Avoid the tendency to please multiple donors with various requirements and be ambiguous about your results strategies. You should be the first to profit from your results and the learning that comes with them.

2. *People.* Focus on building staff or volunteer capacity to look at data and its broader implications for the organization or project. Build up people's confidence and equip them with the proper training to get data

collection and analysis right and on-target. But, when hiring people, love for data should be secondary to understanding the context. Remember: context is ever evolving in a social world that determines and closely dictates what methods and strategies are appropriate. Continuous learning is the engine of always-improving staff or local volunteers.

3. *Measurements.* Most organizations and individual leaders neglect their own organizational need for evidence-based insights they can use right away. A one-person development initiative can start and end in a straightforward review process devoid of complexity. The what, when, where, who, and how elements of simple reporting are a good start, but there are several methods and techniques. Choose the light, forward-looking approaches that best suit your situation. Mine formative lessons that feed into current work, rather than top-heavy, summative mechanisms prevalent in the sector. And when you get into the summative review, without budget or staffing support, be clear on your evaluation needs. From there, simplify your sampling process. Use reliable secondary information that's readily available. Use the mixed-methods approach (qualitative and quantitative) to increase the validity of your findings.[2]

4. *Resources.* Breaking down the results-orientation framework will highlight the need for resources to budget for the other three elements: people, strategy, and measurements.

A regular organizational results review is critical as a mechanism to revisit and reinvent past work, considering emerging developments and challenges in a fluid social environment.

Explaining Your Impact: Causation, Correlation, and Attribution

Now that you're aware of the need for a results orientation, it's time to look at your impact explanation—that is, how your inputs connect to impacts that are observed in your change partner and the broader society.

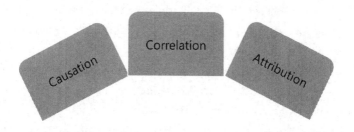

Figure 7: The Impact Explanation

Causation

The gold standard is causation, though there has been an ongoing debate about causation as the way forward. Some think nothing compares to its rigor and validity. Others claim it's merely part of the spectrum, evidence of the continually evolving need to connect our inputs to the changes we seek. Most of the time, you don't need causality. A robust impact explanation that addresses validity questions is good enough.

Claiming causality requires substantial evidence. Causality means that, without your interventions, those changes wouldn't have taken place. If the changes you intended happened, how did different demographics among your change partners (i.e. men, women, children, the disabled, the elderly, etc.) enjoy the benefit? Gender and equity are intersecting issues in evaluating impacts, as are other variables, such as effectiveness, efficiency, impact, sustainability, and relevance.[3]

Tracking changes with partners who have been with the program for several years is relatively doable. The complexity increases when there are more partners at higher levels of societal change. Randomized controlled trials (RCTs) are typically used to arrive at cause-and-effect explanations. The method reduces bias by having a randomly selected control group and the "treatment as usual" group, comparing effects within a set period.

RCTs are expensive and time-intensive. They aren't for everyone. However, RCTs can be effective and less costly if governments and other partners have data you can use right away. There are methodological and political controversies surrounding experiments with controlled and uncontrolled populations. Use RCTs when causation is a non-negotiable requirement, above other considerations, to meet users' needs.

An example of an RCT is the Government of Ontario's Basic Income Pilot launched in 2016. The Ontario government tested how basic income supports could help people living with low incomes meet their needs while improving key socio-economic outcomes such as mental health, education and training, and housing stability.[4] The report became the basis of the broader consultations in 2017 which led to the Ontario Basic Income Pilot project which runs for three years with up to 4,000 participants receiving payments.

Correlation

According to the *Canadian Oxford Dictionary*, correlation means "to have or show a certain relationship." You can correlate your inputs with other variables to show that other variables are at play that you don't have any means of controlling. One change in the variable doesn't mean or lead to a change in another variable. Claiming correlation doesn't mean causation. Still, you can use correlation to account for the (non-)linear relationship with other known and measured variables (i.e. social or cultural norms, a leader's influence, etc.).

Esther Duflo and Lucia Breierova's 2004 study on the impact

of education on fertility and child mortality confirmed the earlier literature on the significant relationship between the two. The study found that female education is indeed more important in determining the age at marriage and the number of children before the woman turns 15 or 25. However, it does not confirm that female education has more of a causal impact on a child's mortality than male education.[5]

Attribution

Attribution theory comes from social psychology, and considers how people explain their and others' behaviors using psychological or external causes as a determining factor.[6] You attribute your inputs as one cause of the changes you observe in your partner. This explanation is modest, and you can use attribution as a means of underlining the limitations of the study.

Attribution science has gained traction in recent years to establish the link between human activities and climate change. Using computer models and data, researchers simulate scenarios that could account for climate change in the present as a means by which to anticipate what future situations could entail.

Causation, correlation, and attribution as plausible explanations of your impact require a scientific method to arrive at conclusions. Causation requires more rigor than the other two. Anecdotes and stories aren't good enough. You must be committed to the accepted principles of social research, grounded in qualitative and quantitative, corroborating lines of evidence. Counterfactual evidence will make any explanation more robust.

Your choice of explanation depends on your need for validity, the assumptions you've made about your work, and the level of rigor you require as part of the accountability piece. Resource limitations will also inform the review process, and the availability of evidentiary support for your claims. Remember, no one will expect you to show precise causality. Each organization is unique, and even if there are guidelines and standards to adhere to, use your best judgment within the options available. Emerging creative approaches to explaining your impact, ones that are context-specific and methodologically agile, could be useful alternatives. For example, life histories can be useful where grassroots, people-to-people interactions occur on a regular basis and significant social meanings can be derived.[7]

Here are four steps to ensure your impact claims are consistent with your overall results strategy:

1. *Adopt a developmental orientation.* Your evolving frameworks match your abilities and confidence in implementation. Know what is going on in terms of good practice and pursue the right fit for your situation.

2. *Don't start from an evaluative perspective.* Evaluation evokes feelings of fear and inadequacy. Begin the process with continuous improvement as an aim and innovation as a proactive engine. No one's job or reputation is on the line.

3. *Invest in the back end of the process and start low and slow.* Develop capacity and engagement with the change partners: this is crucial. You are clearing away real and perceived obstacles on the ground by doing this.

4. *Beware of the science and politics of your claims.* The risks are plenty if you compromise the accuracy of your process. Political aspects are at more serious risk of fallout if not adequately girded. Avoid surprises by communicating the broader implications of your results in advance to high-level stakeholders.

Why Spin the Wheel That's Lost Its Thread?

We do things by rote without considering that some practices have lost their power and relevance. Individual and collective initiatives become repetitive and lose their potency to affect change in the long run. When frustrated with the results, it's time to question the operating model that sets the parameter of your actions.

Leaders can get sidetracked with grand ideas that have no real practical value for partners. Community work has become factory-like—a complete assembly line of ground-level projects and staff scrambling to fill every area with a flurry of activity after activity. Elsewhere, a factory of funding proposals aims to keep the team on payroll and prevent the organization from closing. Leaders chase money predictably attached to the next shiny object, which could be machine learning, artificial intelligence, or cryptocurrency. Many actors still subscribe to this model because they think there is no alternative.

An impact-driven orientation flips the development model on its head. It puts value right at the heart of any initiative.

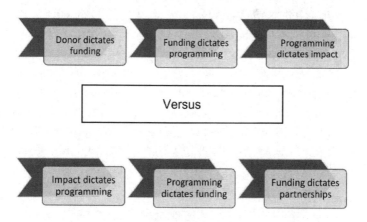

Figure 8: Development On Its Head

In a 2018 DEVEX interview, former First Lady of Afghanistan Rula Ghani put this dilemma well: "Why don't they stop and look at the model of the NGO? It's the most unsustainable model because it goes cycle by cycle. Once the cycle is finished, the NGO has to go with its begging bowl and get more money. If they were doing agriculture and the money is for medical, well, they'll become medical specialists. And if the money is for handicap, they become handicap specialists. What kind of model is this?"[8]

An international organization based in British Columbia, Canada, shared on social media that they had tried many things: microfinance, food security, climate change adaptation, community-based resource management, gender-based violence prevention, and maternal health, among others. They ultimately discovered it's best to focus on their core mission of reducing poverty through a holistic-development approach, using education, health, agriculture, and gender equality.

Three signals tell us we need to stop chasing butterflies and focus on providing more value and impact as results:

1. When your inputs don't move the needle on a micro or a macro scale, it's time to *get back to your primary mission* and concentrate on where you could make a vast difference. In short, be so wildly excellent that no one can ignore your work.

2. *Stop applying band-aid solutions* when surgery is more appropriate. Multi-sectoral partnership actors in the aftermath of the 2013 Rana Plaza tragedy in Dhaka, Bangladesh, which killed 1,100 garment factory workers when a building collapsed, used a multi-pronged approach to preventing future accidents by securing accountability across the global supply chain.

3. *Work within your systems*—networks, alliances, and organizations that can support your work and the results you want. Working within systems brings coherence, provides more reasons to collaborate, and finds synergy through multiple-angle perspectives.

Declare War on Waste: Four Strategies
for a Results Mindset

A results mindset is the best antidote to overreach, cutting waste, and focusing on efficient action. Here are four strategies to declare war on waste to get results:

1. *Simplify the complicated.* Instead of a 25-page project report, ask yourself what information and insights will improve your work. The lessons can be shared and inform the work of others. Pick three strategic lessons and three practical lessons. This rule applies to everything else in your spokes.

2. *Keep the essential front and center.* Education and training are a common strategy for development. However, if these activities have no bearing on real, tracked-and-measured performance objectives, the mere acquisition of knowledge doesn't automatically translate to changes in the field.

3. *Support organic ideas.* Believe in your partners and communities. Look inside for the gold, fill the gaps, and strengthen competence. Use homegrown models of best practice and inspire local people to follow those leads.

4. *Act swiftly.* Invest in quick learning loops and timelines that call for immediate deployment of insights. Taking stock shouldn't take an enormous amount of time. Time-to-market is more important than the idealized benefits of slow meditation.

There are many ways to count and measure impact. A results orientation makes a world of difference to a provocateur, in a sea of naysaying critics and evidence-based fanatics. Sure, results provide technical accountability. But they're also good business sense. And they're the hallmark of an individual or organization with robust, high-performing initiatives. Adapt the conventional rules to what works in your context and own up to the political and social consequences that come from communicating your outcomes.

Summary:
Reflective Questions Using the Global
Impact Leadership Framework

In the space below, reflect on the questions using the 5Ps—Purpose, Passion, Provision, Practice, and Paradigm—as bases for being strategic in measuring and communicating results.

- What impact claims will be the best vehicle for articulating your outcomes? How can you best articulate your results for a given project?

- How do you ensure a results orientation throughout your engagement with a project and beyond, as a capacity-building investment?

- How can waste manifest in your work, and what strategies have you found effective in dealing with it?

Principle 7

Empower Your Defenders
through Your Story

The seventh principle for global impact leaders is to share your stories authentically and powerfully, to increase support and build community. It all starts with your personal story, which connects others to your sense of purpose, your journey toward self-discovery, and your vulnerability. In an environment full of noise, exploitation of the Other, and pseudo-truths—and whether working as part of an organization or doing it alone— you need a compelling, authentic vision, a real-life narrative emphasizing the singularity of your message.

After a few months of recovery from a failed attempt on her life, Malala Yousafzai addressed the United Nations (UN) on a girl's right to education:[1]

Dear brothers and sisters, do remember one thing: Malala Day is not my day. Today is the day of every woman, every boy and every girl who have raised their voice for their rights.

There are hundreds of human rights activists and social workers who are not only speaking for their rights, but who are struggling to achieve their goal of peace, education and equality. Thousands of people have been killed by the terrorists and millions have been injured. I am just one of them. So here I stand. So here I stand, one girl, among many. I speak not for myself, but so those without a voice can be heard. Those who have fought for their rights. Their right to live in peace. Their right to be treated with dignity. Their right to equality of opportunity. Their right to be educated.

Dear friends, on 9 October 2012, the Taliban shot me on the left side of my forehead. They shot my friends, too. They thought that the bullets would silence us, but they failed. And out of that silence came thousands of voices.

The dream of Malala is now that of anyone who wants to make a better world through education of girls and women. Inspiring and powerful, Malala's message of nonviolence has galvanized millions to act in peace, forgiveness, and the relentless pursuit of good.

There Are Countless Stories, and Yours Matters

Stories are a tool for humanizing the theories, frameworks, and concepts the development sector uses to try to create a better society. Nothing quite resonates like a well-told personal experience because it gives people a chance to see themselves in your vulnerability, mistakes, and grace.

Backstories in particular are potent engines for authentic conversation and collective action. They humanize the teller amid a culture of trash talk, social-media distraction, fake news, and instant experts. The world is hungry for real leaders who ignite action and inspire generations to stand up and be counted, an antidote to the online culture of vicious personal attacks that represents a staggering decline in civility and civic consciousness.

Stories bring hope and inspire change. We cannot leave public storytelling to political leaders and others in high-level positions who use stories to gain popularity for self-interest. We cannot rest on the so-called influencers to inspire us.

As a global impact leader with passion, purpose, practice, provision, and paradigm, you can bring thousands of people to your journey, struggles, and triumphs, not for voyeurism in the Big Brother tradition, but in the name of true solidarity toward shared, evolved purpose. People look up to leaders for their capacity to inspire as much as for their competencies or ability to do great work.

Is storytelling performative, theatrical, and self-serving? Not necessarily. Provocateurs will have no qualms holding the microphone and staying in the limelight. They'll relish it because their message is bigger than who they are.

Call them sages, philosophers, prophets, poets, teachers: every storyteller has a different way of communicating their message through their life and stories. But any effective storyteller will be motivated by quality. Three things to keep in mind:

1. *Quality of the message.* The strength of your convictions and the passion with which you pursue your goals despite adversity will affect your story. There is no question that some ideas travel like wildfire and some melt in the heat of the sun. People appreciate messages that provide value, ignite hope, positivity, and kindness, and offer concrete resources for applying a process, skill, or experience. Don't be the impact leader who uses stories of communities to dehumanize and rob them of their dignity.

   Sponsorship infomercials depicting children in dirty, impoverished conditions with flies hovering over them still exist and should be banned. Not only do they perpetuate the idea that these children need saviors from developed countries, but they use children in need as nameless, voiceless commodities, often without the consent of their parents or guardians.

2. *Quality of the medium.* Which medium best supports your vision? How can you reach the people you need to be working with? The medium is the message, and different media attract different groups. Consistency and quantity over perfection build connections and credibility.

3. *Quality of the messenger.* Be a trustworthy communicator. The messenger usually gets shot first, so build stamina

for unfiltered comments. Only you understand your own unique power to share your vision with the world. It doesn't matter if you didn't finish college, don't know English, and didn't read classic literature. Can you share your story in your language with the rest of the world? If you can do that, you can inspire thousands of people by just being you. Malala Yousafzai stood tall as this type of leader, bold enough to be who she was and what she represented, to the point of courting death.

Your Story's Followers: Fans, Acolytes, and Defenders

- *Fans* are the base camp of followership in a new media-focused environment. They can be clueless social-media followers, or have a loose connection with your programs. Whatever attracted them to your cause or project, they need constant information to stay engaged. Fans can turn into acolytes or enemies. They may be of interest to your organization or cause, but also constitute sheer engagement numbers, with transitory interests and changing expectations. They may advance their commitments to you with the right understanding, tools, and mechanisms.

- *Acolytes* have a certain investment in their relationship with you. They've donated at least once or advanced your agenda in ways that can be tracked. They can use their purchasing or network power to advance your agenda. They are convinced they want to be a part of your movement and will take steps with their resources to register support. Acolytes are ready to receive how-to tools so they can help, without getting in the way.

- *Defenders* are loyal followers who will—not with blind faith—walk in your shoes, eat at your table, and travel with you when you ask them to. These are dedicated champions invested in your work and connected to your goals. They want to succeed with you. Best of all, they're there for the long haul (see Principle 3). When you face problems, they take you up on solutions and provide problem-solving you may not see. Defenders are on committees and working groups; they provide structural support and volunteer their time.

The concept of loyalty and followership has evolved radically over the last 20 years. Recent literature on followership also notes how the quality and nature of leadership spawns a certain type of followership. Followers are now more influential and strategic than ever before. They will continue to exert an enormous amount of power as leaders recede from view, or simply respond to what strong followers demand from them.

"If you build it, they will come," a saying from the 1989 film *Field of Dreams*, is a fallacy. No one will buy, donate, and give their time if they don't know about you and your message first. Cultivating your supporters is mission-critical. Converting your fans to defenders is the goal. The ultimate test for defenders is the continuity of their loyalty, with or without you. Successful organizations long survive their founders or originators, and their original ideas.

Beware of false followers as you would false prophets. Both are a dime a dozen. Internet gurus buy social-media ads and followers, mesmerizing their audiences with the appearance of instant success, fame, health, Zen, debt-free lifestyles, wealth, more. Ignore them.

The Command of a Singular Idea

Your story's command of a singular idea is the sharp, powerful point of your message's arrow. Global impact leaders cannot risk being drowned out by the noise of social media and the dumbing down of culture. Your idea should shine through clichés and misinformation.

Provocateurs are different from scientists, consultants, speakers, academics, and bloggers. They're not about branding and positioning. They're 1% of the entire population because they sing a different tune that resonates across many global sectors and disciplines. They speak with integrity and have a large arsenal of backstories that make them influencers in the authentic sense of the word. They won't back down from an honest debate, carefully choosing which arena works best to overturn a popular idea, without going overboard.

You can stand out from the crowd with the value of your story. A local police officer started blogging to promote anti-bullying in schools, using his own experience of bullying at a young age. Youth from different countries reached out to him and posted comments on his website about their experiences, asking for help to cope with mental anguish, negative peer pressure, and suicide ideation. He was invited to speak to a youth organization based in the United Kingdom on anti-bullying programs that work. Your audience may not be the world or even a sizable number from your community, but every person who is helped through the value of your message is a significant win.

Confidence, Originality, and Strategy

Make an impact through your stories by keeping the following values in mind:

- *Confidence, not humility.* Believe in yourself to deliver a true message of hope and inspiration. Humility for the sake of being loved, admired, or accepted is a counterfeit trait. It's not appropriate when there's work to do. Impact leaders do not need external validation or to be adored.
- *Originality is the best influencer.* Your story can stand out

easily in our contemporary culture of unoriginality. If you're the 200th person to use the same logic or jargon on social media, you're part of an echo chamber. People want to hear actual solutions and strategies they can use now. If you ask them to check out your webinars, seminars, TEDx, podcasts, or blogs, be responsible for managing the responses that come after.

- *Strategy informs the message.* Any messenger is as good as their strategy. What's the bottom line? Are you creating a superstructure for your work that will ultimately take over? Are you building a movement where each member is as good as the whole? Do you want the public to donate to your cause? Do you want to effect policy change in your local community? Hundreds of young millionaires have thousands of followers for their products and ideas, but their business interests take precedence. You don't want to be just another nonprofit looking for financial support, or some bored philanthropist who had nothing to share except leftover money.

- *Cut through the noise to create support.* Keep yourself above partisanship, petty debates, and the artificiality of social-media popularity. Focus on your key message and give value to your main audience. You will create a cadre of genuine supporters who believe in your vision.

- *Own your story.* Resist being diluted and pushed aside. Speak to your supporters both formally and informally, online and in-person, to create actual conversations without digital mediation. Being original and out-of-the-ordinary could attract thousands of fake followers who will keep your message diluted and turn it into a cliché. These are the so-called curators, weavers, and documenters. They have nothing of value to add to the discourse, so they regurgitate it.

- *Don't play the charisma card.* The last thing you want to be is pleasant, compliant, and a pushover, but charismatic leaders of all dispositions play on magnetism and appeal to generate support for a trendy, esoteric, or flavor-of-the-month movement that will dissolve before it gets any traction. Personality-driven actions are rarely sustainable.

- *Act on what your audience values the most.* The key to successful storytelling, winning support, and gathering loyal followers is bringing value to what an audience appreciates the most. Stories, images, appeals, campaigns, writing—all bring clarity and purpose to your messaging. When there is a clear fit between your vision (or your organization's vision) and your audience's values and wants, you become the voice and face to a cause that is dear to their hearts.

Connect, Check, and Protect

The following three story-building strategies can help you retain the best people to support your important work:

1. *Build a consistent connection with your audience.* Define what's valuable for that specific group and treat them as your allies in your impact journey. Pick the media through which you can communicate with them regularly.

2. *Check your facts.* If people will be donating or investing in your projects, be accurate with your stories and reports. Stick to truthful narratives and attribution so that you can support your ideals through evidence.[2]

3. *Protect your brand.* Whether it's your organization or your own brand as an impact leader, learn to keep things professional, yet personable. Separate casual likes or dislikes from your personal worth or that of your organization.

Summary:
Reflective Questions Using the Global
Impact Leadership Framework

In the space below, reflect on the questions using the 5Ps: Purpose, Passion, Provision, Practice, and Paradigm.

- Where do stories figure in your work as a global impact leader? What's the story behind your work?

- What minefields and pitfalls should you avoid when building a connection through the power of your stories? Or the stories from the work of your organization?

- How can your stories help others be inspired and challenged to come alongside you on your journey?

Principle 8

Envision the End You Intend

The eighth principle for global impact leaders is acknowledging there's no forever in this field. It's healthy and advisable to exit gracefully and effectively. Live your legacy now, through ambitious objectives you can meet within a given time, or throughout your life. It's the gift you give yourself. To avoid undoing hardwon gains on the ground, think about what you want to accomplish before you leave your partners. Then, work backwards.

Sam is the founder and director of a nonprofit community organization based in Ontario. He led the organization to national prominence, making lasting, positive impacts in the lives of thousands of communities. Over the past ten years, he garnered major national recognition, becoming a household name and source of pride for his community. However, charges of corruption and conflict of interest hounded his last years as CEO and founder. Divisions occurred among his team and loyal supporters. The organization fragmented, and programming suffered. The media highlighted everything that went wrong. Sam's sacrifices and outstanding work for over three decades diminished overnight. His followers withdrew their support. Following advice from his lawyers, he retired, waiting for a vindication of his legacy.

If you've been a founder, president, or partner and haven't taken a leave or a different role since your appointment, chances are you're overstaying your welcome. You're probably becoming part of the problem. Remember: you're in a change field! Many warn against staying in one place for too long, and for good reason. Not heeding the call for change can reverse your gains and hurt your relationships. Protecting yourself from yourself requires a brutal assessment of when it's time to go. Whether collaborative, a partnership, or community-based, start any relationship with the end in mind. The knowledge you will leave one day gives you perspective before taking the plunge. Your intervention will always be short, because needs are expansive and resources are finite.

Live the Legacy You Can Be Proud Of

A true legacy is not something you leave when you die. Legacy is about *who you are* and *what you represent right now*. Waiting for death with the intention of leaving something tangible behind to celebrate yourself is a big error.

My grandmother, the wise woman in her community, left nothing behind. She didn't have possessions, immediate relations, or memorabilia to prove she existed and mattered. However, her words of wisdom echo loud and clear in our psyches, 30 years later. She wasn't busy storing items up for posterity. She was busy pursuing her grand objectives and living large. Her memory is truly alive in us.

Age is a question of attitude, and it's just a number. If you are afraid that you are too old to leave behind a legacy unless you plan for it right before your death, think again. It's never too late to achieve what your heart desires. Consider these octogenarians and nonagenarians:

- Anne Teeuwsen, a 90-year-old senior care resident in Alberta, Canada, won a literary award for her memoir. Despite her Parkinson's diasease, she inspired countless writers in the community to pursue their goals in life.
- Karthyayani Amma, a 96-year-old Kerala woman, got a 98% mark in her literacy mission examination and became the Commonwealth of Learning Goodwill Ambassador. She is living proof of learning at any age.
- Kimani Maruge was the oldest primary-school student in Kenya and was featured in the 2010 film *The First Grader*.

He was a Mau-Mau fighter during the British rule in Kenya. The UN recognized his contribution to literacy at 85.

- Yuichiro Miura, an 80-year-old Japanese man, was the oldest to climb Mount Everest and returned alive to tell his grandchildren about it. There is no limit for someone who has strong tenacity to beat all odds.

If you are younger, forget the bucket list of putting up a thousand schools, teaching a thousand indigent children, or eradicating a major disease. Instead of creating a checklist, develop clear life-objectives—a grand design into which all other elements fit. *Live out your goals now rather than expecting to be recognized for your achievements posthumously.*

Consider four types of goal-oriented objectives:

1. *Personal.* This is how you want to live your life, now, not putting off the great work for tomorrow. It's being consistent with your practice and paradigms. What goals will help you grow and mature as a leader, person, and change agent?

2. *Partnership.* This is the relationship between your personal objectives and your partnership. When you're done or have moved on with other things, how do you see the objectives evolving and growing with your initial investment? See Principle 2 for advice on the kinds of partnerships that work.

3. *Institutional.* This is your objective across the sectors in which you work. What can you do to strengthen practice, process, and capacity across the change landscape? How can you, as an individual, create a ripple effect? How can you have a broader impact on communities?

4. *Innovational.* Are there new ways of knowing and doing that others can gain by working with you? How are they able to integrate this new knowledge?

Dependencies, Relapses, and Reboots

A successful exit is similar to your grown-up child moving out. The transition is scary for both of you, but inevitable. As parents, we respect our adult children's choices and decisions, however silly or foolish they may initially seem to us. We hope the years of teaching and training won't be futile. Wherever they go, whatever life's challenges, our children have the tools to overcome them, because of how we've raised them.

Dependencies and co-dependencies are the result of long, unexamined relationships that have atrophied. Stable but unresponsive connections could lead to both partners abdicating their responsibilities, and to challenging one another.

With continued financial, institutional, and industry supports, leaders can quickly become inured to taking a hard look at their current state of affairs and naming the proverbial elephant in the room. Honesty is the best policy in an open, safe, and respectful space, and not observing it can lead to *relapse*, which may occur when change partners return to old, self-limiting views after years of transformative work.

Relapse is an obstacle to a successful exit. Ideally, your change partners will become independent and fully capable of setting their course. But when relapse happens, the second time around is harder, and change partners are more resistant. Even when there's trust, putting things back again takes ample time and effort. Such setbacks should remind impact leaders to consider people's psyches rather than provide tons of resources. Without the proper change perspective, communities can misappropriate resources.

I have seen communities come from a major intervention and look worse than ever, because the intervention was palliative. Corruption happens, as well as conflict between groups and individuals. Leaders must ask their change partners if they believe they are worse or better off because of the partnership.

Maybe you're both in need of a *reboot*. A reboot involves

looking at a relationship at arm's length and acknowledging the possibilities for further collaboration or working together, whether for short- or long-term initiatives. It's correcting the causes of the relapse and instigating proper accountabilities to ensure that sustainability efforts rest on the leaders, their managers, and the strength of the relationships they leverage.

Reboots can be planned from the beginning, or emergent. World Wildlife Fund in the UK referred to the latter as a "spin-off," a "creative process." Spin-offs could be about a totally new relationship (i.e. not as donor), the creation of a new entity, and self-sufficiency, among others.[1]

Sometimes, rebooting is about identifying the sustainability needs of the partner, so they can bring in external partners. In 2012, the British Red Cross decided to discontinue its long-term relationship with their local partners. After a visit in 2014, they found out that the local organization had focused their attention on resource mobilization and had gone into "survival mode." They decided to postpone the exit to another year, to focus on building capacity for financial sustainability.[2]

Evolve with Your Partners

Over time, relationships should mature. New roles and expectations can emerge at any point, appropriate to the level of leadership and management capacities. You can come alongside to provide mentoring support, or direct change partners to supports that are provided by their peers, who are mature in their roles and immersed in the change partner's own culture.

Another opportunity for an impact leader is to become a partnership broker and networker for the community whose needs have become more complex and multilayered. Involving outsider champions can leverage community knowledge, and hone their skills in dealing with governments, coalitions, and international actors.

Sometimes, impact leaders sit in community groups and

councils as advisors. Here, they offer an external perspective but remain close enough to understand the community's growth needs. In this position, the leader can push the envelope and test assumptions and mindsets.

Either roles can merge or stand alone, depending on both parties' joint vision and risk appetite. There is no expectation to become someone else or do something out of obligation. Relations can continue regardless of how development unfolds in the future.

Four Strategies to Exit Gracefully

1. Plan the plan

Provocateurs prepare to leave from the start, knowing it's healthier for all concerned. Communicating timelines and building capacities are the cornerstones of a successful departure. While some leaders refuse to make a timeline because of technical, funding, or implementation issues, it's better not to leave things to chance.

INTRAC, a UK-based organization, has been tracking the experiences of nonprofits withdrawing aid since 2012. Most of their action-learning results show that, to be responsible, exits should be embedded in the wider organizational culture and systems. While INTRAC focused on larger and more established nonprofits, individual impact leaders can benefit from the lessons of building exits into their program design, partner relationships, and capacities, albeit on a much smaller scale.[3]

The longer you stay, the longer the likelihood of creating dependencies, and "overdoing" development. While no number is ideal, most leaders benchmark five to ten years as the limit for engagement. Capacity building becomes an embedded strategy when you stage the exit as a natural progression. Leave on a high note, not waiting for a climax or dramatic event.

2. Avoid the pitfalls

Goodbyes are hard, but inevitable. Execute your withdrawal timelines with tact and respect. Consult and include traditionally excluded groups such as women, young people, and people with disabilities proactively in decision-making. Build back forward.

Before exiting, be clear on achievements, and the work to be continued. Be clear on new arrangements. The change partner should know what to expect, what the dissolution brings, and what will remain the same. There shouldn't be any ambiguity between the old and the new. Mixing the two creates confusion and skewed expectations.

Transition to self-governance or self-empowerment could be hit-and-miss. Expect that the community will need more resources to create a path forward to their goal, and fill the gaps, thus necessitating a bridging project or initiative. The community's long-term capacity objectives are more likely to be fulfilled if you employ help from allies. Celebrate this need to generate positive feelings of togetherness while recognizing the vast opportunities ahead.

World Vision Tanzania's phase out from the Chipanga Area Development Programme based in central Tanzania did not translate to actual sustainability of benefits. Their late transition to an exit, their lack of managerial, technical, and leadership capacities, and their financial uncertainty about the local organizations that assumed responsibility, as well as an absence of concrete resource generation, were the main reasons.[4] All of this can be avoided if exit strategies are woven into a plan two to five years before the termination date. Systematically assess and make concrete activities that will build capacities and resources.

3. Build leadership capacity every step of the way

Provocateurs, in deep relation with their change partners, view every intervention and interaction as a teaching and training moment. Prepare community leaders to carry on with their roles with a more strategic vision for the future. The people are the facilitators, catalysts, and owners of their development agenda.

Build the capacity of the groups for when you leave, particularly the disproportionately affected populations. Build the capacity of local experts to come in and help with the transition. Fortify the leadership capacities of community elders, advisors, and informal allies as protective assets against reversals.

Unlearning is different for every individual, and far more difficult for a team and an entire community. All learning relationships should start with unlearning and relearning. Communities are best at learning from the example of others. Your example matters the most.

To complement an audit when the partnership starts, you can conduct an exit audit to identify gaps in your partner's organizational self-sufficiency. Tracking these competencies results in a clear picture of the increases in capacities, and where they will have problems. The people will welcome this opportunity to learn while you exit.

A Better World Canada has an assistant executive director in place to take over for one year while their projects end. Their exit principle includes providing training, skills evaluation, and for the local partner, a strong commitment to the cause. They are willing to cultivate new donors, until these donors build relationship with new leadership.

4. Reimagine the future

Moving on can signal the birth of a new relationship. The high of the exit process can lead to a peer-level friendship shaped by learning and sharing. Both sides may enjoy a new sense of awareness and solidarity. Bring in new tools and resources to grow the community.[5] Use new ways of connecting and leading that don't require your presence.

Harry Schmidt wanted one thing: "I need to see the faces of the children." A housing contractor in British Columbia, Schmidt built several children's shelters in many countries. He cared deeply for the people and organizations with whom he worked since their first shelter project in the late 1980s. On a trip to Ukraine in 2005, he told some young adults, "You must never forget where you came from. You must never forget the poor who did not have the opportunities you had. One day, you will have the resources to share with others. I am getting old and one day will drop out of the picture. I cannot come and help people."[6] Passing the baton can catapult all involved to a greater sense of purpose. Your legacy is not physical infrastructure, but your impact and your message.

Provocateurs understand that it's not too late to build a legacy by living your large objectives now. For some, exits are truly the end of the relationship. For others, exits are part of the evolving dynamics between the impact leader and the change partners. There's no hard and fast rule. Take time, give it care, and know that an exit marks the commencement of the next phase.

Summary:
Reflective Questions Using the Global
Impact Leadership Framework

In the space below, reflect on the questions using the 5Ps: Purpose, Passion, Provision, Practice, and Paradigm. Remember, the 5Ps provide you with criteria to exit gracefully and inspire your partners to carry on the work with excellence.

- What would you do differently knowing that legacy is not something you leave behind but something to live fully now?

- Have you ever witnessed a change leader who stayed too long? What were the negative impacts? What have you learned from your observations?

- Exits can be a powerful and transformative experience that will inspire partners to become better leaders and individuals. How can exits be used to increase the leadership capacities of your change partners?

Principle 9

Find and Nurture Your Community

The ninth principle for global impact leaders is to find and nurture your community, because transformative journeys are never solitary. A provocateur relies on global communities that collaborate on a vision and build bridges across geographic, linguistic, political, and cultural divides. The drive to localization in development reaps greater dividends when the fruits of prosperity, sustainable growth, and economic development are pushed to the margins.

Mothers can change the world. Jessica James, founder of Social Good Moms, started blogging in 2002 when her daughters were small and a couple of years later started Mom Bloggers Club. This was back when companies would work with bloggers and provide them with sample products and services as part of their promotions. When One Organization, an anti-poverty initiative co-founded by Bono, invited James to Kenya in 2008, she realized blogger moms can make a difference.

Social Good Moms worked with nonprofit organizations such as Oxfam and the Gates Foundation promoting their campaigns on maternal health and women's issues globally. Through their thousands of members, they supported campaigns, fundraising efforts, and information drives of partner organizations to amplify messages and rekindle support for women's health and well-being. Since its founding in 2012, the initiative has had a global reporting system where members travel to different parts of the world and report back findings from partner projects. To date, there are 3000 members in 30 countries and their blog posts reach over 500 million people. In an interview, James said, "NGOs were sometimes talking to themselves. The idea of Mom Bloggers for Social Good was to get other people to do the talking for them."[1]

Even the "Beggar" Needs to Belong Somewhere

A friend once said to me, "Even 'beggars' need to belong somewhere." There are many partnerships and connections that you can foster in your quest to find meaning through your passion, purpose, practice, provision, and paradigm. Encouraging a sense of belonging is a huge part of your development work as a provocateur.

Being part of something larger than yourself is an essential growth trait. Because of this, those at the forefront of change should be wired to connect in deeper ways: to sustain and grow their humanity, regardless of the shape or type of these interactions. Although there are many associations and networks that promote the holistic potential of individuals, it's ultra-critical to find the right ones and keep with them. Finding the right associations and networks is not easy. With the contemporary idea of community predicated so much on online and social media, as well as in-person commitment, there are many entities competing for your attention, with not a lot of differentiation.

I considered myself a reluctant social-media user and digital citizen for many years. Nowadays, I have strict rules for using social media such as Facebook and LinkedIn, and digital-business communication platforms such as Slack, to connect for personal and professional needs. And yet, I find myself in the rabbit holes of these interfaces, losing a lot of time lurking around. If you're not careful, there's enough loopy content to keep you away from your important agenda.

Belonging is a vital human need. Impact leaders must choose between getting their needs met through an association or creating that association themselves.

Not all associations are equal. Some associations have become irrelevant and circular in their approach to today's complex work. Some associations are struggling to keep up with membership in a time when identification with a certain profession or club is the only motive. The true value of association is not in continuing education, networking, certifications, or event discounts, but in being competitive, current, and relevant in the contemporary economic and social environments, where banding together has more advantages than going alone. Global impact leaders forging their path cannot risk being saddled with associations that have typical, traditional, and tedious administrative requirements.

That said, you're only as good as your association, and it's better to go it alone than to suffer from the lack of imagination of a given group. It's a waste of time and money to be around those who lie about their successes and blame the government or regulations for their industry's deficiencies or for their professional woes. Consider traditional charity clubs, whose memberships are dying or already dead. Their causes are great and honorable, but they are failing to attract the middle careerists and emerging impact leaders who are hungry to be taken up for community causes they can be proud to work on. Given that professionals have careers, families, and other interests that are holding them up, clubs cannot compete with these obligations, and lose their edge by insisting on their weekly Tuesday meetings, quorums, and other perfunctory requirements. Clubs are only as good as the passion of their members.

During the COVID-19 pandemic especially, associations have had little recourse but to cut costs, cancel big events, and migrate quickly to online platforms to continue to provide services for which they've become known, and to engage their members. The future of the traditional association will be bleak, however, unless they transition back to a more responsive, mobile, and forward-looking model, rather than just transferring existing models online. If members now expect to design and decide which services they want, associations must specialize in exclusive, high-value offerings. They can't be all for all members.

What does belonging look like, then, if traditional setups aren't sufficient? As a provocateur in the global space, you should use the Global Leadership Framework to guide you in how you decide to affiliate. Are associations that interest you aligned with their purpose? Do they offer an equal measure of challenge, growth, and flexibility, encouraging members to become active co-creators? In terms of insights and perspectives, do they provide the right environment for you to find your voice and leadership style? Will they become a source of mentors, advisors, and peers you can trust and rely on for real-time advice and supports? Will you be proud to hang out with them outside the formal events? If yes, then this could be the association with which you can have long-term satisfaction.

How you affiliate also depends on your mileage, your experiences, and where you want to be in the next five to ten years. Some leaders prefer to be in a small, mastermind group to exchange best practices, fine-tune a new skill or habit, or build accountability around certain commitments. Whatever it is, it's what's pressing that should be the focus of your investment. You might find global networks are just as productive and interesting as those in your backyard.

The so-called beggar already has their group. They have intelligence systems to get free food, shelter, clothes, and the best places to panhandle. They share information among themselves on weather, traffic, and crowds coming and going. If they belong somewhere, so do you!

Cyber Communities and the Return to the Personal
Recent community-building perspective claims that cyber communities cannot take the place of in-person communities. This is not necessarily the case. Cyber communities can be as effective as in-person communities, and sometimes even better at getting things done.

From 2003 to 2007 I was a part of an international organization with memberships from over ten countries. We met once a year as a collective to hold our annual general meeting and conduct our business. Throughout the year we did our planning, visioning, task-force setup, writing, and other essential tasks virtually. Every year, we accomplished a lot more than most in-person associations in most countries.

What was the secret? Because we didn't have face-to-face interaction, there was an enormous amount of trust-building at the beginning of the relationship. There was a vetting process to ensure alignment in values, principles, code of conduct, and ways of effective remote working.

We confided in each other as peers, and trusted each other to carry out assigned tasks using feedback, constant validation, and a system of communication and leadership. It was not a perfect system, but it worked for our mission. We felt connected and supported every step of the way. When we finally met, there was an entire year of working together online that enabled us to become even more cohesive as a group.

Every year, new networks and organizations form. Their audiences come from anywhere in the world. While registered in one country, an organization can hold a cross-border audience and have a distinctly international character. In Canada alone, the list of international organizations has widened because of the capacity to travel, work virtually as a team, produce outstanding outputs across various time zones, and command a following from any place in the world: whoever cares about and aligns with their causes, values, and dispositions.

Cyber communities are the products of a hyper-globalized and digital-first environment. These working communities do not just exist on platforms like Facebook. We can bridge the divide through voice, text, graphics, and video conferencing. During initial COVID-19 lockdowns, seniors at care homes were being taught how to videoconference to connect with loved ones. Companies that refused to allow some employees to work from home had to succumb to public-health regulations. Most international organizations were converted to virtual work seemingly overnight. Research on the evidence of the use of cash transfers in communities required shifting quickly to online, using mobile phone surveys to gather data.[2] As a society, we have reached a learning curve both unprecedented and critical.

There are many things we can do with our digital capacity, yet it also presents opportunities for those who want to build on the long-standing, sustainable community practices that have always been effective. I believe in the saying that usually accompanies a tech glitch: "technology is good when it works." The latest technologies can complement the practices of community-building by, for instance, the use of smartphones to get real-time feedback from partners, the use of Zoom and other online meeting tools to get boards to make time-sensitive decisions, or the use of satellite feeds for situational analysis of hard-to-reach areas. Technology should amplify the great work being done without supplanting or subverting its purpose. When applying technology for routine use or complex operations, it is important to educate the users and end-receivers, thereby increasing its contextual relevance and fluency.

There is an incorrect assumption, given the attachment to technology in Western youth culture and professional life, that digital connection is the norm. It is important for provocateurs to realize their change partners may not have the same access they do. The majority of developing countries continue to experience a digital-progress imbalance. Many parts of Africa, Asia, Latin America, and the Caribbean have slower connections and high mobile-data costs. Climate volatility will have an impact on energy availability and cost, which will adversely affect Internet availability and effectiveness.

While we venerate what we can do with our smartphones and googling, I believe there are tremendous misses entailed in not being able to touch a person, pick up subtle hints from an embodied reaction, and convey thoughts and feelings without saying a word. Presence makes us feel more alive and connected. Engaging communities in dialogue, showing how things work with tools, and sharing new knowledge requires in-person connection. A smile, a handshake, a gesture to receive an invitation for tea or snacks with a host are all simply irreplaceable. Breaking bread together is not just a customary practice for communities but also a social need, and an abundant experience for cohesion and belonging.

Five Tips for Joining, Creating, and Nurturing Communities

1. *Real communities are not about rules, protocol, and more rules.* They are about authentic and aligned interests and ideas, about themselves and the world. Communities are born out of need, but they seldom grow because of the superimposition of values from a leader or outside force. They form from a set of beliefs about what they can do, how they will do it, and move from there.

2. *Real communities have their ups and downs.* When starting a community, beware of the need to be something you or your organization is not. The best community is driven by big, ambitious goals beyond organizations or platforms that have the simplest but clearest call for action. If the organization is calling for a radical change with a pie-in-the-sky action agenda, it's hard to get buy-in for even the fence-sitters. Anya Hindmarch's 2007 "I'm not a plastic bag" campaign[3] went viral globally because of a simple ask: for consumers to change their plastic bag habits to reusable canvas totes instead.

3. *Real communities transform the people within them, and the organizations that form them.* The community will go where there is real passion and commitment, and where directions are clear and unhindered. It becomes a self-

112

generating mechanism, with all involved making value for all to consume, at the same time—making sure a community's "why" remains relevant throughout its existence.

4. *Real communities can go beyond borders, nationalities, languages, political persuasions, and personal proclivities.* There should be a real intention to learn from one another's diversity and viewpoints and to share a common thread, even without agreeing all the time on all the points.

5. *Real communities test themselves for authentic leadership.* Leadership provides the strategic direction and the environment where it can thrive. Leadership should be revolving, with everyone taking ownership of successes and failures. When followers only follow and do not take the lead at any level, they pull the community down. Free-riders and spoilers make a community costly to run and manage.

Transformative Journeys Are Contagious

People traveling on the same plane, bus, jeepney, or tuk-tuk will likely bump into each other and find out they share many commonalities aside from going to the same destination.

As a global impact leader, your destination will not define your specific legacy contribution or the number of accolades you will accumulate. It may be a cliché that it's the journey that counts, but most impact leaders I interviewed for this book recalled their most productive times as those when even the people closest to them didn't believe in their dream.

When you are just beginning, nobody seems to hear or listen to you, or even give you 15 minutes of their time. This is when reality sets in. All your passion, energy, and enthusiasm cannot survive without attending to your business, professional practice, and personal issues as well. You are bootstrapping a dream that will enable you to help other people live better lives.

Being invisible when you start out is a blessing. You're not prematurely exposed to the whims and politics of the industry. It's a protective shield: just concentrate on doing great work no one can ignore. Premature success leads to dead ends. Those who rise quickly without the sound foundation of the 5Ps usually fall under the weight of their falsities or grow lazy quickly, thinking they've "arrived." When you're ready and you have a quality body of work, you're prepared to confront other actors and will enjoy trading and cooperating on tangible, actionable ideas immensely.

In my early twenties, I rushed to build a career in international development so that by my thirties I'd get those coveted positions that involved higher pay, travel opportunities, more training and development, prestige, and a greater chance to use my skills and talents. I told myself that if I had enough skills, talents, and potential, people would see me. Why was I continually treated as if I had nothing to contribute? I longed for opportunities to expand and grow into a professional to be reckoned with. I was ready to learn the ropes, work in the field, and deliver great results. However, I informally sought mentors who weren't for me.

By my thirties, I had gained a position that enabled me to rise above the challenges of the job and proved my leadership skills in more ways than one. The position also gave me the experiences I cherished and enjoyed. The last five years of my thirties were very productive and challenging, and allowed me to become a better human being and professional.

Looking back on two decades of work, experiences, and lessons learned, I believe opportunities come when you're ready. I was totally under the radar publicly, and when I finally used my name for my consulting business, it felt dreadful. These two decades were preparation for the larger work ahead: consulting, speaking, authoring, and teaching, all spokes in my expertise wheel, always reinforcing one another.

People You Meet along the Way

Within a spectrum of practices, fledgling impact leaders can benefit from a low profile when it's the learning that counts. Here are three types you're likely to encounter on your journey:

1. *Cynics*. This is the person who's "been there and done that" and will tell you that your destination isn't good, because the area is polluted, underdeveloped, the people aren't that friendly, the food is awful, and so on. They can't wait to discourage you. They think they're doing you a favor by telling you to stop and turn around before you run into more trouble. Families and close friends can subtly and injuriously do this.

2. *Enthusiasts*. The second group will tell you that your destination is the best thing in the world. They enjoyed it tremendously and would go back, given the chance. They describe your destination as one of a kind, an oasis, heaven on earth, and give you some real tips you can use when you arrive. They'll give you their maps, a souvenir item, and offer to connect you with their local operator for some good deals. Better yet, they'll tell you to try everything once. Be your own judge of their advice.

3. *Neutrals*. The third group doesn't have an opinion about the destination. They've heard what others have done and seen what impacts are possible. They're neither hot nor cold. Their advice: if this is what you're trying to do, there might be ways to do it without breaking the bank, running into emergency health issues while traveling, having a bad time, and so on. They have secondhand information, confirmed or from the grapevine. They

can't resist connecting you with someone they know who has done similar work or something close to it.

You will encounter these three groups all the time, especially when starting or scaling up. Each has their truth to tell but not the entire puzzle. Judge for yourself and, as a rule, ignore unsolicited advice.

Stay Close to Kindred Spirits

Transformative journeys are contagious because fellow provocateurs like you are orbiting a different space, sector, or industry in a parallel fashion. They have the same understanding of the 5Ps, and a flair for provoking change and inspiring action. Walking with them even for a few minutes will be worth your time. Some will stay for an entire season, enabling you to compare notes and commiserate. Fellow provocateurs also help you to be human and relax with your imperfect self.

In Principle 3, I talked about playing the long game and anticipating uncertainties along the way. I have just talked about being part of a community that's true to your calling and aligned with your growth aspirations. When your journey gets tough and no association or groups can help, however, to whom do you turn? This is where the group becomes important. Everybody loves success, but failure is an orphan. When failure happens, you'd better be in the right company—around people who will tell you what you need, not what you want, to hear.

Provocateurs seldom have a cadre of minions who go with them as shock absorbers or enablers. For the most part, they travel alone, not needing validation or confirmation. Sure, they like good company. But if it's not the right fit, they're not afraid to walk alone.

Tying the Knots of Impact—from the Center to the Margins

Let's go back to the community you're building with your change partners.

The work of community-building depends on your agency, and your ability to make sense of a situation and to generate a community's sense of intelligence and wisdom. Everything I have seen working in developing countries is because there's a community standing up for itself and fighting tooth and nail to make things better for their generation and the next.

Localization means many things in different contexts. Opposite to corporate adaptation is a localization where development gains pour down to local communities and the benefits of material, technological, political, social, and human-resources innovations are pushed to the margins. Change partners should be able to make their own decisions about development that meet their own needs and aspirations, and that expand their own repertoire of possibilities. Localization's objective should be to protect and rebuild local economies worldwide.

A Community-First Model for Localization

Localization is an alternative to corporate globalization's control of agriculture, food security, employment, and livelihoods. Thousands of local communities have sprung up to create viable and sustainable food production, empowering women and marginalized communities to enhance food security and protect environmental legacies. Local farmers' markets, for instance, running on buy-local campaigns, are pragmatic responses to globalized food production, distribution, pricing, and marketing. Other examples include local business incubation projects, circular procurement, crowdfunding and crowdsourcing, thrift stores and upcycle projects, old-fashioned cooperatives, buy-local and city-wide procurement schemes, community gardens, barter-type exchanges, and so on.

Localization is about the direction of power. It relocates and recalibrates benefits, advantages, and power to the people at the local level. It is about control and sovereignty. Local communities harness what they have, build sustainable structures, develop their human capital, increase entrepreneurship, and collectively negotiate for better policy outcomes with their governments. A colleague in a meeting of peacebuilders once said, "You will never have power unless you create your food." My father-in-law, a third-generation farmer, knew the value of growing crops to feed his family and animals for years. He ensures that bins are full, and, in case of emergencies, the harvest can feed a family or two for a year. There is still a barter system among many farming and farm-based communities, enduring as a practice for centuries.

When considering economic sovereignty, global impact leaders must know the bigger picture of conflict and contestation. In many developing regions there are imbalanced trading practices and norms that alienate those who are already voiceless and powerless. Provocateurs must take part in the discourse at the community level or their efforts will be thrown by the wayside because of the magnitude of the issues beyond their control. Anti-globalist rhetoric is useless in the face of the pressing needs of local communities. It does not, in any shape or form, forge a pragmatic way forward to help developing communities achieve agency.

The poor are being transplanted, manipulated, and brainwashed to become professional protesters, willing to sideline positive changes within their families, groups, and societies. I knew a family who suffered from having both parents be part of the protest movement, always in the streets and rarely at home. During election season in the Philippines, all the political candidates have their representatives from marginalized sectors function as allies and the "true voice of the people." When one of them wins the election, the other groups coalesce to unseat the winner from office, claiming they are the "true voice." Politics often sows division in developing communities.

As an impact leader, you must expect that your journey will be non-linear, complex, and very unpredictable. It is a major achievement if you've been successful in finding your own professional community. Ultimately, however, you are bringing the benefits of community-building to the local level, where small ripples can create massive change. You are as good as your community.

Summary:
Reflective Questions Using the Global
Impact Leadership Framework

In the space below, reflect on the questions using the 5Ps: Purpose, Passion, Provision, Practice, and Paradigm.

- Imaginative communities can create the environment for a virtuous circle, the opposite of a vicious cycle, where good things lead to more good things. How do you nurture and grow your community of like-minded peers and provocateurs?

- Where do you draw inspiration, mutual support, and camaraderie in times of self-doubt, uncertainty, and stress? What types of advice would you give young provocateurs who are looking to find their own community?

- How can you champion localization as a principle and strategy for action in its many representations in the lives of your change partners and communities?

Principle 10

Dare the Impossible

The tenth principle for global impact leaders is to dare the impossible. Reap the rewards of trailblazing. Your role is to help democratize innovation and institutionalize creative expression, so communities get better at solving their own problems and addressing their own weaknesses. Failing to meet this challenge is, without a doubt, a major reason several social-good efforts fail.

Dr. Hawa Abdi, described by *Glamour* as "equal parts Mother Teresa and Rambo," led an exemplary life as a doctor, humanitarian, and darer of the impossible. After the civil war broke out in Somalia, Abdi at one point housed 90,000 displaced persons on her land, providing medical care, food, and water. Abdi's endeavor was fraught with risk. She was held hostage in her hospital. Her camp was always vulnerable to raids by warlords. Women and girls feared being raped. At one point there was no food for the people. Once, a businessman backed by Al-Shabab evicted the displaced from Abdi's land. Another time, boys with guns came and tried to take over the management by right of their gender, to which Abdi retorted: "Even goats have two testes. What have you done for our society?"

Looking at the big picture, Abdi wasn't content just to take care of the medical needs of these refugees. She also founded a farmers' market as part of the women's entrepreneurship program, along with a high school and a vocational program.

When Abdi went to Uganda to introduce her work to Ugandans, they offered her land. She said, "I have shelter, water, hospital, food, [and a] vocational school. I [would] need these all in Uganda." The Ugandan government replied, "We can't. We are government. You need the United Nations to do that." Abdi then said: "[But] I am one woman, and I did all that."[1]

Massive challenges have been confronted and overcome because provocateurs like Abdi dared not let the seemingly impossible paralyze them and prevent them from acting.

Don't Get Lost in the Weeds—Hold Your Head High

Global impact leaders cannot afford to get lost in the weeds. Their productivity demands purpose, their legitimacy performance, their popularity integrity. Because provocateurs are "uncategorized non-state actors," they cannot afford to behave like a nonprofit (although they may have one) or assume they must do what other big institutions do, because of the protocols and accountability mechanisms imposed on all actors.

Inspect and investigate who's done it before, and what went wrong. Many times, when trying something new with a community where previous experiments have already failed, there is a "been there, done that" mentality. Unless a community is presented with recent evidence of positive and transformative results, they will not be open to risks for their own sake. Poor people are tired of being used as guinea pigs in development projects and trials. They want a solution they can 100% own. If you are presenting a technological or data-based solution, consider building a strong foundation with users and adapting to local culture and inclinations. The hard-tech solution may be plunking down another satellite dish in a community or training people to use a new computer program. But don't underestimate soft tech: ensuring people understand the uses and benefits of technology, and how to become good stewards and owners of it.

Take the case of local ownership of wells built in Africa. Local ownership is not just providing training for local mechanics. It's setting up systems of distribution and payments, and monitoring these regularly. It's ensuring that hardware can be procured locally at affordable prices and that suppliers exist in the region. In short, there must be local economic ecosystems to support any initiative.

Not All Innovation Is Equal

Development projects are increasingly entrepreneurial and innovation oriented. Business enterprises for social good and even large development projects of multilateral institutions are now characterized by nimbleness, resistance to red tape, quick product turnaround, short feedback loops, and light environmental and social footprints. With globalization and the rise of available data, there is differentiation, localization, customization, and adaptation. Organizations must have rapid reiteration protocols with less lag time to market. Less bureaucracy means greater citizen services that, at their best, are affordable, appropriate, and accessible.

Provocateurs need to democratize innovation and systematize imagination, so communities get better at solving their own problems and addressing their own weaknesses and limitations. Leaders in communities should co-design and co-invest in experiments involving solutions to complex challenges that no one entity can sufficiently resolve. Global impact leaders facilitate this process by questioning orthodoxies, cultural resistance, and political convenience.

There are many spurts of innovation in the development sector that provocateurs need to examine and rethink. There are management, technological, implementation, cultural, and social innovations. Sadly, aside from a few success stories, there are many epic failures in crossing last-mile poverty thresholds. Many policymakers and practitioners still face the dilemma of how to integrate what's already working well with the richness of the local content. Technological innovations, as an example, have low uptake if the design does not consider the local user, and networks and business ecosystems are delinked.[2]

Innovators must keep in mind the robust local network of extended families, neighbors, and friends who could be early adopters and supporters. They also need to understand, support, and strengthen local business ecosystems. Due to aggressive marketing, solar panels have been popular in many households in East Africa. When solar panels broke down, however, there were very few local repair shops that could fix them. Many abandoned the use of solar panels entirely. Many organizations attempted to introduce efficient cooking stoves with clear health and environmental benefits for the poor. Yet, because these stoves varied in affordability, accessibility, and efficiency, their uptake had lackluster results.[3]

It's Not the Poor—It's the Lower Middle Class

The conduit for successful adoption of innovation is not the poor and the voiceless, but the lower middle class. This group can help the global aid and development movement know which services, products, and ideas get to the poor faster, more conveniently, and with more affordability. The lower middle class have a lived experience of poverty. Through education, technological knowledge, market awareness, and cross-border communications, they have improved their material prospects.

Take the case of overseas Filipino workers' families. They have used international knowledge, connections, technology, and of course remittance, to send their children to school to get degrees, have better jobs, and develop into informed better citizens. The net effect is dramatic.

Overseas workers have a global outlook, international skills and work ethics, and are heralded as "new heroes" by their governments, which rely heavily on them to keep their economies afloat. All overseas foreign workers, no matter if they hail from India, Nepal, Bangladesh, Indonesia, Nigeria, and so on, have the same stories of struggles and hardships. Recent literature on global remittances and the impacts on families and communities reports that consumption patterns are skewed toward education, livelihood or business enterprise, and modern-day necessities such as cellular phones, Internet, cable TVs, and computers that can facilitate instant global communication with their loved ones.

Overseas workers' families benefit from income supplementation that provides for basic necessities, but also encourages business activities that can support their long-term needs when their relative comes home for good. When you walk around a rural community and see modern houses with two to three floors, in-house toilets, and garages for two cars or more, predictably, there is a relative working abroad who made this possible.

Families of overseas workers are early adopters within their communities. They can spread innovations that will indirectly benefit even the poorest of the poor. The explosion of mobile money services in East Africa, for instance, transformed the economic and social lives of rural communities. The leading telecommunication providers in four countries in East Africa tapped into the already globally connected families of overseas workers who needed fast, efficient, and hassle-free money transfers directly through their cell phones.[4] Soon enough, cheaper cell phones and pay-per-airtime modalities increased connectivity, even in the most remote locations. Mobile connectivity brought rural people out of isolation and, with this, brought knowledge, strategies, and connections to increase economic opportunity.

Democratize Innovation Now!

We must democratize the space for innovation. Small organizations, low-level grantees, and grassroots communities must have a voice in these developments. They are closest to the problems. The idea that you've got to conform or be swallowed up does not work at the local level, where trust holds sway and is necessary for individual and collective survival.

With all the hype about the technological future, ordinary people and local populations should be able to understand, participate in, and contribute to innovations that have a direct impact on their lives. No techies can afford to ignore more than half of the global population living in developing countries as potential users and animators of these products.

Here are five ways to democratize innovation in developing countries:

1. *Raise the bar* of performance, products, services, or any offering of the organization. Don't get comfortable or stay stagnant. Improve as you go. Learn from the successful organizations in the field and adapt what works.

2. *Encourage communities* to design their own programs and invent their own tactics. Failing is better than not trying at all. The license to fail is the same as the creative license: artists express themselves, question norms and standards, and interrogate certain given realities. Invest in your change partner's search for solutions without putting pressure on them for immediate success.

3. *Use crowdfunding* to experiment, knowing that those who firmly stand behind your ideas can share the risks. The crowdfunding phenomenon has released monies and capital from having to be tied to specific institutions, organizations, or governments. Crowdfunded initiatives can be as independent as they want to be.

4. *Scale out* before you scale up. Your change partners don't have to use innovation on a massive scale. Innovation at an organizational level is worth aspiring to as well, and it is a mark of genuine commitment to outcomes, regardless of size, growth, and aspiration.

5. *Produce equity-seeking results* by aligning scarce resources and initiatives. Dole-outs, handouts, charity giving, and tied aid have limited utility. Invest in people.

Worlds Colliding! Are You Ready?

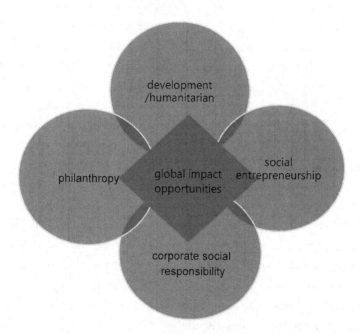

Figure 9: The Interstitial Opportunities for the Global Impact Leader

Social entrepreneurship start-up culture is predicated on scaling up fast and using imagination and innovation to stimulate fresh thinking in the field. The nonprofit sector is preoccupied with disseminating best practices widely, ensuring sector leaders learn, and benefits trickle down to the served populations. Businesses are attempting to integrate sustainability into their corporate strategies.[5] The philanthropic sector is experimenting with social finance, investments, and green vehicles.

Philanthropy, development, social entrepreneurship, and corporate social responsibility at the global level are colliding. Borders are becoming more porous, and each field is being disrupted and is disrupting at the same time. No one field can claim it holds the keys to eradicating poverty and other problems. Cross-pollination and borrowing are the orders of the day.

The promise for global impact leaders lies in the interstices of these domains as spaces to tinker, tamper, and trailblaze. Collaborations and partnerships must rise from the ground up. Businesses and development organizations have been working together on a global scale since the United Nations' Millennium Development Goals, but there have been fissures, contradictions, tensions, and massive differences in perspective and approach. There are also gaps in value systems, missions, and power differentials, which, often, are irreconcilable. Few are bold enough to venture into these interstices because it's uncharted territory. There is danger and risk. Only the well-prepared succeed.

Provocateurs as global impact leaders can be the gap-fillers, influencers, and connectors here. They come from the business, government, philanthropic, and social-enterprise sectors and can act as interpreters and meaning-makers, uniting diverse actors through the overriding mission of sustainability. The strategic insight of provocateurs can be used to diminish conflicts and inherent incompatibilities of these unnatural partnerships.

Practical partnerships can happen while philosophical differences get sorted out. Right now, when the chips are down, there's no choice but to work together.

The Rewards of Creating Your Pathways to Innovation and Breakthroughs

There are roads well-traveled in the business of poverty alleviation and overall social development. You don't want to go down there. Provocateurs create their own pathways. While innovators subscribe to the latest combinations of data, technology, and development science, impact leaders aggregate and synthesize this new knowledge based on what works and what gets ultimately supported.

Because your projects and initiatives do not require outsider approval and other people's monies (OPMs), there's no other entity necessary to legitimize your ideas. This is emancipating from a transformation perspective. It's also critical when work on the ground requires the long game. While non-state, individual actors are either crucified or hailed as providing "manna from heaven," you can focus on real success.

But there are blueprints we can rely on. The Ramon Magsaysay Award Foundation, Asia's equivalent of the Nobel Peace Prize, extols the best, brightest, and most successful champions of development in Asia. Since 1965 these awards have given us a playbook for what to expect, what works with communities, and how solutions can be widely shared in other regions of the world. Whatever the region, insights are available, ready to be integrated and acted on. Experts often do it over a lifetime commitment that outlives flaky pseudo-humanitarians and self-proclaimed heroes.

We are all change-makers, in our own right, but not all of us can become effective game-changers.

Game-changing is about reframing the scope and parameters of engagement, and playing on your strength. Game-changing doesn't require a lot of brain power, talent, or connections. It doesn't require you to shift lanes or careers or jobs. It doesn't require lots of capital infusion. Game-changing for global impact leaders is performing at the big-picture level and increasing impact at the local level. It's being connected to what's going on and deeply aware of both constraints and opportunities.

To be a game-changer is to use intersectional and multidisciplinary approaches. Weave your way into these worlds that are conspiring for the better. Be ready for a surprise. You could end up working on something more impactful than what you had initially assumed was a sure thing.

It's time to do it. Take advantage of redirecting local energies and creativities to achieve better and greater results for the communities that need them.

Summary:
Reflective Questions Using the Global
Impact Leadership Framework

In the space below, reflect on the questions using the 5Ps: Purpose, Passion, Provision, Practice, and Paradigm.

- As an impact leader, how can you support creativity and innovation with those who have few resources but, nonetheless, talent, hard work, and ingenuity?

- How can you increase the adoption and integration of innovations in disadvantaged communities?

- How do you imagine becoming a game-changer rather than a change-maker in your field?

Conclusion

Come Full Circle: Global Impact Leadership in Turbulent Times

Our highly disruptive times, just like the times before us, call for fortitude and innovation. Lisa, Cidalia, Risa, Calvin, Eric, Jennifer, Abdi, Malala, and many more mentioned in this book offered unique, unconventional contributions. Acting in the face of moral decay and injustice is not about forced choice. We can choose to be courageous when it's not comfortable, or even safe.

COVID-19 has transformed how we work, live, do business, and connect as human beings. We have yet to see the full magnitude of the fallouts from lockdowns, which were undoubtedly more harmful to economies and societies than the disease itself. Given pre-pandemic economic recessions in various parts of the world, recovery is ongoing, and will be difficult.

For the altruists among us, there is a sense of overwhelm. We face so many problems: the global refugee crisis; climate issues and ecological devastation; instability of global markets; global terrorism; moral degradation and spiritual decline; wars, genocide, the arms race, weapons of mass destruction; political and ideological polarization; identity-based injustices and oppressions (racism, sexism, injustice, and inequality); mental-health issues such as depression, anxiety, and suicide.

These massive challenges threaten the major achievements we've made in technological, educational, industrial, political, and socio-economic arenas. Yet, there are many powerful acts of kindness and generative work to celebrate and fortify.

Many silent heroes are doing great work. New actors, groups, networks, and movements are created every year, tackling global and local problems with surprising precision and professionalism. There are recent, creative, and non-traditional approaches to fostering inclusion, belonging, and well-being in development. Local soup kitchens have become immigrant soup kitchens. Restaurants are owned by veterans and people with disabilities. Vertical community gardens are on the rise. Many collective, autonomous efforts are driving change into society's peripheries.

Clearly, two favorable driving forces will accelerate the work cut out for the provocateurs.

With the middle classes expanding in Africa, Asia and the Pacific, Central and South America, and other regions, with hyper-globalization and the mobility of workers, social entrepreneurship will become more significant. Environmental, health, and development challenges will require a combination of mass consumer response, corporate involvement, and government support. Regional provocateurs continue to make themselves heard, breathing fresh air into overcrowded, heavily aided regions whose needs they know intimately. *Provocateurs from all walks of life, anywhere in the world, engage with social entrepreneurs for social and economic transformations.*

Principle 10 outlined how global diaspora movements have enabled the tighter linkage of countries, regions, and economies. They are uniquely positioned to traverse borders and strengthen people-to-people connections in the development field. They sit on boards, committees, and task-forces for local service clubs, think tanks, and government consultation bodies about their countries of origin. They inform and shape bilateral policies including, but not limited to, trade and commerce, education, health, technology, political affairs, and security relations. In the last decade or so, more diaspora groups and individuals have taken matters into their own hands, going beyond giving back by setting up businesses and social enterprises, and entering innovation challenges to maximize the potential of transferring expertise and global mindsets to local talent back home. *Provocateurs consult and invite diasporas back into their communities using their local knowledge, international perspectives, remittance, know-how, heritage and culture, and help in disasters.*[1] *They will be a stronger force for good for years to come.*

The Future Agency of the Global Impact Leader

This book is nothing less than a manifesto: ten principles of global leadership that will help you make an extraordinary difference, one initiative at a time. My no-nonsense guidelines apply to individual change agents, whom I call provocateurs, in various organizational and community settings. Through the 5Ps—Passion, Purpose, Practice, Provision, and Paradigm—provocateurs can reinterpret seemingly intractable problems and explore promising solutions with insight and imagination. It won't be an easy ride.

Principles are important but abstract. The principles in this book are attached to real-life experiences. The principles are designed as practical, living frameworks, ready to be interpreted by aspiring provocateurs in the face of evolving social mores and political considerations. The more you apply the insights in this book on your own, the more they become part of your leadership toolkit.

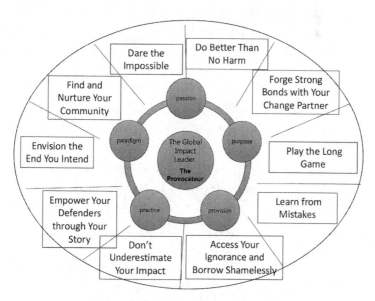

Figure 10: Tying It All Together: The Global Impact Leadership Framework and the Ten Principles

The field is vast. Good intentions can quickly go awry. Measures that do not account for the context, futures, and aspirations of those we are trying to help simply don't hold up. The movement toward lifestyle humanitarianism is on the rise. Some call it celebrity-, theatre-, and/or performance-based spectator humanitarianism. There are not enough constructive responses to redirect these efforts. This book offers refreshing, practical encouragement.

Global impact leaders believe there are always options, alternatives, and discoveries waiting to be applied. Yes, there are many ready-made solutions. But it's vital to find the applicable and smartest routes to breakthroughs.

When you're running out of steam, here's how to find and recenter your courage, self-awareness, pragmatism, and skepticism:

- *When low on Purpose, turn to Principles 6 and 8.* Think about defining and building your legacy now. Before you go overseas, consider how you can offer the best contribution to your local economy and society, and to the families, neighborhoods, and groups with whom you collaborate.
- *When low on Practice, turn to Principles 3 and 5.* Expose yourself to the realities of your projects and partners, and learn with humility.
- *When low in Provision, turn to Principles 7 and 9.* Invest in the right resources and people; it starts with you.
- *When low in Paradigm, turn to Principles 1, 2, and 4.* Think about how you can build relational accountability, and outcomes you can be proud of.
- *When low in Passion, turn to Principle 10.* Get down and dirty. Follow your gut and don't wait for the perfect situation to get involved.

Organization, institutions, and industry leaders: you have the power and influence to effect these changes now. Some key ingredients for change:

- *Senior provocateurs.* There are massive coaching and mentoring opportunities, but they will require more mentors. Neither mentor nor mentee will need a rule book: mentors, give your mentees high-level mandates, and set them free.
- *Robust infrastructure.* Knowledge diffusers and human-capital development accelerators are needed to nurture the next cohort of leaders. We need more health, development, and environment interlinkages, not in implementation but in developing talent pipelines to meet the immense recovery and preparedness needs.
- *Innovative education.* The next university degree in development could be an experiential program where students learn from communities, on the ground. Their teachers would be experts in flood mitigation, child nutrition, planting sea gardens, and more: artisans, farmers, disaster survivors, those among the rural and urban poor, and social workers.

Readers, your journey in global impact is just beginning. I invite you to keep in touch with me at www.maidenmfrank.com, in my present role as Global Impact Advisor. Share your successes and ongoing challenges so I can help move you in the right direction. Together we can spread positive provocation and contribute to post-pandemic emergence at the grassroots, local, national, and international levels.

There will always be everyday humanitarian leaders among us. I believe in harnessing the power of the individual in a networked economy and globalized society to become a force for good. Provocateurs, not philanthropists, exemplify the best in humanity. Provocateurs represent the most expansive kind of human thinking. Our times call for tinkering, tampering, and transformation in the service of others. I celebrate that. Step up and be counted.

References

Introduction

1. United Nations Volunteer (UNV) (2021) 'State of the World's Volunteerism Report: Building Equal and Inclusive Societies,' Bonn (Online) Available at https://swvr2022.unv.org/ (Accessed 1 April 2022).
2. Volunteer Canada (2018) 'Volunteering Counts: Formal and Informal Contributions of Canadians in 2018' (Online) Available at https://volunteer.ca/vdemo/ResearchAndResources_DOCS/Webinar%20Presentations/Volunteer_Canada_GSS%20GVP_June%2014_EN.pdf, 5 November 2021.
3. Social Security Administration (2012) 'Annual Performance Plan for Fiscal Year 2012 and Revised Final Performance Plan for Fiscal Year 2011 Report' (Online) Available at https://www.ssa.gov/performance/2012/APP%202012%20508%20PDF.pdf, 21 March 2022.
4. Children International (2018) 'Global Poverty and Giving' (Online) Available at https://www.children.org/global-poverty/global-poverty-facts/facts-about-world-poverty-and-donations, 5 May 2020.
5. Fechter, A. M. and Schwittay, A. (2019) 'Citizen Aid: Grassroots Interventions in Development and Humanitarianism,' *Third World Quarterly*, 40(10), pp. 1769–80. doi: 10.1080/01436597.2019.1656062.
6. Tomlinson, B. (2016) 'Small and Medium-Sized Canadian Civil Society Organizations as Development Actors: A Review of Evidence,' *Inter-Council Network* (Online) Available at https://icn-rcc.ca/wp-content/uploads/ICNSMOStudy_May-24.pdf, 20 May 2021.
7. Duflo, E., Banerjee, A., & Horbeck, R. (2018) 'How Much Do Existing Borrowers Value Microfinance? Evidence from an Experiment on Bundling Microcredit and Insurance,'

Economica, 85(340), pp. 671–700.

8. Bass, B. M. and Avolio, B. J. (1993) 'Transformational Leadership and Organizational Culture,' *Public Administration Quarterly*, 17(1), pp. 112–121.

9. Cleveland, H. (2002) *Nobody in Charge: Essays on the Future of Leadership*. 1st edn. San Francisco: Jossey-Bass.

Principle 1: Do Better Than No Harm

1. Sadler, J. (2010) 'A Hard Blog Post to Write...1MillionShirts,' *1 Million T-Shirts* (Online) Available at http://1millionshirts. org/blog/a-hard-blog-post-to-write-1millionshirts/ (Accessed 10 November 2021).

2. ABS-CBN News (2020) 'Criticisms on Manila Bay beautification "misplaced," only P28-M spent for white sand,' *ABS-CBN News* (Online) Available at https://news. abs-cbn.com/news/09/12/20/cost-of-manila-bay-white-sand-project-dolomite-dilg-denr, 31 December 2021.

3. Bishop, M. and Green, M (2008). *Philanthrocapitalism: How Giving Can Save the World*. New York: Bloomsbury Press.

4. McGoey, L. (2015) *No Such Thing as a Free Gift: The Gates Foundation and the Price of Philanthropy*. New York: Verso.

5. Crawford, J. (2021) 'Does Bill Gates have too much influence in the WHO?' SWI swissinfo.ch (Online) Available at https:// www.swissinfo.ch/eng/politics/does-bill-gates-have-too-much-influence-in-the-who-/46570526 (Accessed 14 September 2021).

6. General, R. (2019) 'Chocolate Biscuits From Spain Called "Filipinos" Spark Controversy Again in The Philippines,' *Nextshark.com* (Online) Available at https://nextshark. com/spain-chocolate-biscuits-called-filipinos/ (Accessed 28 November 2021).

7. A Better World Canada (2020). 'About: The Story of A Better World' (Online) Available at https://www.abwcanada.ca/ about-us/ (Accessed 13 January 2020).

Principle 2: Forge Strong Bonds with Your Change Partner

1. Djiofack, C. (2021) Unpublished interview conducted by Maiden Manzanal-Frank, 15 January.
2. Aspen Roundtable (1998) 'Nothing as Practical as Good Theory' (Online) Available at http://www.aspenroundtable. org/vol1/weiss.htm (Accessed 3 November 2021).

Principle 3: Play the Long Game

1. Redvers, L. (2019) 'Searching for the nexus: It's all about the money,' *The New Humanitarian* (Online) Available at https:// www.thenewhumanitarian.org/special-report/2019/12/3/ triple-nexus-aid-development-humanitarian-donors-coopera tion?msclkid=45b10cc4aa4f11ecb8b89c5cd5a9325b (Accessed 12 October 2020).
2. EvalPartners (2015) 'We refuse to eat shit,' *Evaluations that make a difference* (Online). Available at https://evaluationstories.files. wordpress.com/2015/11/evaluations-that-make-a-difference-en_21sep15.pdf (Accessed 30 November 2021).
3. Gold, R. (2021) Unpublished interview conducted by Maiden Manzanal-Frank, 21 July; Miracle of Help Home Page (Online) Available at https://www.miracleofhelp.org/ (Accessed 30 November 2021).
4. Nir K. and Jeffrey V. (2018) 'Blockchain in Developing Countries,' *IT Professional*, 20(2), pp. 11–14. doi: 10.1109/ MITP.2018.021921645.
5. SAP International (2013) 'How Big Data and Social Mapping Aid Typhoon Haiyan Efforts,' (Online) Available at https:// blogs.sap.com/2013/11/20/big-data-to-the-rescue/ (Accessed 14 December 2020).
6. McAfee, A. and Brynjolfsson, E. (2012) 'Big Data: The Management Revolution,' *Harvard Business Review*, (10)60–6, 68, 128.
7. Hildebrandt, A. (2013) 'Typhoon Haiyan creates testing

ground for crisis mappers,' *CBC* (Online) Available at https://www.cbc.ca/news/world/typhoon-haiyan-creates-testing-ground-for-crisis-mappers-1.2462119?msclkid=29f0 e5ceaf9f11ec97eafb0f7081771c (Accessed 29 March 2022).

8. Mulder, F., Ferguson, J. E., Groenewegen, P., Boersma, F. K. & Wolbers, J. J. (2016), 'Questioning Big Data: Crowdsourcing crisis data towards an inclusive humanitarian response,' *Big Data & Society*, 3(2), pp. 1–13. https://doi.org/10.1177/2053951716662054.

9. Bornakke, T., and Due, B. (2018) 'Big-Thick Blending: A method of mixing analytical insights from big and thick data sources,' *Big Data & Society*, Sage Journals, 5(1).

10. Heath, D. (2020) 'Reducing Homelessness through Upstream Thinking,' *Public Magazine*, 1 August, pp. 40–3 (Online) Available at https://icma.org/articles/pm-magazine/reducing-homelessness-upstream-thinking (Accessed 10 November 2020).

Principle 4: Learn from Mistakes

1. Rajah, E. (2018) Unpublished interview conducted by Maiden Manzanal-Frank, 30 May.

2. The Guardian (2015) 'Secret Aid Worker: Sexual Harassment in the Industry,' *The Guardian*, 29 July (Online) Available at https://www.theguardian.com/global-development-professionals-network/2015/jul/29/secret-aid-worker-sexual-harassment-and-discrimination (Accessed 15 November 2020).

3. Capobianco, E., Naidu, V. and World Bank (2011) *A decade of aid to the health sector in Somalia, 2000–2009.* Washington, D.C.: World Bank (working paper, no. 215) Available at https://documents1.worldbank.org/curated/en/271421468103478677/pdf/618980WP0Aid0S000public00 BOX358355B.pdf?msclkid=73de10e6ac8711ec9efe3e9529d 8e074 (Accessed 15 November 2020).

4. Andersen, J. J., Johannesen, N., and Rijkers, B. (2022) 'Elite

Capture of Foreign Aid: Evidence from Offshore Bank Accounts,' *Journal of Political Economy*, 130(2), pp. 388–425. doi: 10.1086/717455 which was published as a World Bank Working Paper.

5. Saldinger, A. (2014) 'Sharing failure's lessons,' *DEVEX* (Online) Available at https://www.devex.com/news/sharing-failure-s-lessons-82678 (Accessed 3 December 2021).

6. Barrington, D., Sindall, R., Shaylor, E., and Davis, S. (2014) 'Blunders, Bloopers, Foul-Ups: Sharing Failures in Water, Sanitation and Hygiene Programs,' *Engineering for Change* (Online) Available at https://www.engineeringforchange. org/news/blunders-bloopers-foul-ups-sharing-failures-water-sanitation-hygiene-programs/ (Accessed 3 December 2021).

Principle 5: Access Your Ignorance and Borrow Shamelessly

1. Luis-Akbar, C. (2021) Unpublished interview conducted by Maiden Manzanal-Frank, 5 February. As of April 2022, Cidalia reported that the Taliban occupied the school on 28 August 2021. The same goes for the clinics/infirmaries in Kabul. No news since then.

2. Goldberg, M. L. (2013) 'Typhoon Haiyan in the Philippines Facts and Figures,' *UN Dispatch* (Online) Available at https://www.undispatch.com/typhoon-haiynan-in-the-philippines-facts-and-figured/ (Accessed 2 January 2021).

3. Reyes, R. (2019) 'Yolanda reconstruction still in shambles after 6 years,' *The SUNSTAR Tacloban*, 8 November (Online) Available at https://www.sunstar.com.ph/article/1831107/ Tacloban/Local-News/Yolanda-reconstruction-still-in-shambles-after-6-year (Accessed 21 December 2020).

4. Holland, M., Tucker, I., Mark, M., Kelly, A., and Honigsbaum, O. (2012) 'Africa Innovations: 15 ideas helping to transform a continent,' *The Guardian*, 26 August (Online). Available at

https://www.theguardian.com/world/2012/aug/26/africa-innovations-transform-continent (Accessed 3 November 2020).

5. Sunder, K. (2020) 'The Remarkable Floating Gardens of Bangladesh,' British Broadcasting Corporation (Online). Available at https://www.bbc.com/future/article/20200910-the-remarkable-floating-gardens-of-bangladesh (Accessed 6 November 2020).

6. Day, L., (2021) '15 Creative Waste Solutions', *Citizen Sustainable* (Online) Available at https://citizensustainable.com/15-creative-waste-solutions/ (Accessed 6 November 2020).

7. Corrigan, F. (2020) 'Drones For Deliveries From Medicine To Post, Packages And Pizza,' *DroneZon*, 2 July (Online). Available at https://www.dronezon.com/drones-for-good/drone-parcel-pizza-delivery-service/ (Accessed 25 November 2020).

8. Sternin, J. and Choo, R. (2000) 'The Power of Positive Deviancy: An effort to reduce the malnutrition in Vietnam offers an important lesson about managing change,' *Harvard Business Review*, pp. 14–15.

Principle 6: Don't Underestimate Your Impact

1. McGoey, L. (2015).

2. Bamberger, M. (2005) 'Designing quality impact evaluations under budget, time and data constraints,' *Better Evaluation* (Online) Available at https://www.betterevaluation.org/en/resource/guide/design_impact_eval_under_budget_time_data_constraints (Accessed 14 December 2021).

3. OECD (n.d.) *Development Assistance Committee (DAC)* (Online) Available at https://www.oecd.org/dac/development-assistance-committee/ (15 November 2020).

4. Government of Ontario (2017) 'Government of Ontario's Basic Income Pilot Project,' *Government of Ontario*, 24 April (Online). Available at https://www.ontario.ca/page/ontario-basic-income-pilot (Accessed 4 April 2020).

5. Duflo, E., and Breierova, L. (2004) 'The Impact of Education on Fertility and Child Mortality: Do fathers really matter less than mothers?' *National Bureau of Economic Research*, Working Paper 10513 (Online) Available at http://www.nber.org/papers/w10513 (Accessed 1 January 2021).

6. Wikipedia (2020) 'Attribution' (Online) Available at https://en.wikipedia.org/wiki/Attribution_%28psychology%29 (Accessed 4 April 2020).

7. Appe, S. (2020) 'Beyond the Professionalized Nongovernmental Organization: Life-History Narratives of Grassroots Philanthropic Leaders in Africa,' *Nonprofit Management and Leadership*, 31(2), pp. 335–53. doi: 10.1002/nml.21434.

8. Igoe, M. (2018) 'Q&A: Afghanistan's first lady Rula Ghani wants to build local institutions, not fundraising campaigns,' *DEVEX* (Online) Available at https://www.devex.com/news/q-a-afghanistan-s-first-lady-rula-ghani-wants-to-build-local-institutions-not-fundraising-campaigns-92955 (Accessed 11 May 2020).

Principle 7: Empower Your Defenders through Your Story

1. Ghosh, P. (2013) 'Malala Yousafzai's Speech To UN,' *International Business Times*, (Online) Available at https://www.ibtimes.com/malala-yousafzais-speech-un-full-text-1344117 (Accessed 15 October 2021).

2. Soyer, E. and Hogarth, R. (2020) 'Don't let a good story sell you on a bad idea,' *Harvard Business Review* (Online) Available at https://hbr.org/2020/12/dont-let-a-good-story-sell-you-on-a-bad-idea?utm_source=feedburner&utm_medium=feed&utm_campaign=Feed%3A+harvardbusiness+%28HBR.org%29 (Accessed 17 December 2020).

Principle 8: Envision the End You Intend

1. Hayman, R., James, R., Popplewell, R., and Lewis, S. (2016)

Exit strategies and sustainability: lessons for practitioners. Special Series Paper No. 1. Oxford: INTRAC (Online) Available at https://www.intrac.org/wpcms/wp-content/uploads/2016/11/Exit-strategies-and-sustainability.-Lessons-for-practitioners.-November-2016.pdf#:~:text=In%20February%202014%2C%20INTRAC%20began%20facilitating%20an%20action,Red%20Cross%2C%20EveryChild%2C%20Oxfam%20GB%2C%20Sightsavers%2C%20and%20WWFUK%29.?msclkid=6c6b23b3adee11ec90c8d3c1d500c916 (Accessed 1 January 2022).

2. Hayman, et al. (2016).

3. Hayman, et al. (2016).

4. Mkomagi, J. V., Namwata, B. L., and Masanyiwa, Z. S. (2015) 'Exit strategies and sustainability of local institutions in Tanzania: Experiences from World Vision Tanzania in Bahi District,' *Rural Planning Journal*, 17(1), pp. 17–29 (Accessed online 1 January 2022).

5. Hoogendorn, B. (2018) Unpublished interview conducted by Maiden Manzanal-Frank, 29 June.

6. Schmidt, H. and Coggins, J. (2006) *The Incredible Dream*, Abbotsford, BC, Canada: Schmidt Family Foundation.

Principle 9: Find and Nurture Your Community

1. On the Dot Woman (n.d.) 'Jennifer James: Moms Blogging for a Cause,' *On The Dot Woman*, 2 August 2014 (Online) Available at https://onthedotwoman.com/woman/jennifer-james-moms-blogging-for-a-cause (Accessed 1 January 2021).

2. Harvard Kennedy School (2020) 'COVID-19: Effects in Developing Countries,' *Harvard Kennedy School* (Online) Available at https://www.hks.harvard.edu/more/about/leadership-administration/deans-office/deans-discussions/covid-19-effects-developing (Accessed 16 December 2021).

3. Hindmarch, A. (n.d.) I'm Not A Plastic Bag | Anya Hindmarch UK (Online) Available at https://www.anyahindmarch.com/

pages/im-not-a-plastic-bag?msclkid=33549788ae3c11ec9f67
4b4a8f5a5101 (Accessed 16 January 2021).

Principle 10: Dare the Impossible

1. Bedell, G., (2014) 'Mothers of Innovation,' *Family Innovation Zone* (Online) Available at https://media.nesta.org.uk/documents/mothers_of_innovation.pdf (Accessed 6 October 2021).

2. Khavul S. and Bruton G. D. (2013) 'Harnessing Innovation for Change: Sustainability and Poverty in Developing Countries,' *Journal of Management Studies*, 50(2), pp. 285–306. doi: 10.1111/j.1467-6486.2012.01067.x (Accessed 28 December 2021).

3. Khavul and Bruton (2013).

4. Muwanguzi, S. and Musambira, G. (2021) 'The Transformation of East Africa's Economy Using Mobile Phone Money Services: A Pragmatist Account of ICT Use,' University of North Texas (Accessed 28 December 2021).

5. Porter, M. E. and Kramer, M. R. (2006) 'The link between competitive advantage and corporate social responsibility,' *Harvard Business Review*, 84(12), pp. 78–92 (Accessed 27 December 2021).

Conclusion: Come Full Circle: Global Impact Leadership in Turbulent Times

1. Shivakoti, R. (2019) 'When Disaster Hits Home: Diaspora Engagement After Disasters,' *Migration and Development*, 8(3), pp. 338–54. doi: 10.1080/21632324.2019.1565383.

CHANGEMAKERS BOOKS

Transform your life, transform *our* world. Changemakers Books publishes books for people who seek to become positive, powerful agents of change. These books inform, inspire, and provide practical wisdom and skills to empower us to write the next chapter of humanity's future.
www.changemakers-books.com

The Resilience Series
The Resilience Series is a collaborative effort by the authors of Changemakers Books in response to the 2020 coronavirus pandemic. Each concise volume offers expert advice and practical exercises for mastering specific skills and abilities. Our intention is that by strengthening your resilience, you can better survive and even thrive in a time of crisis.
www.resiliencebooks.com

Adapt and Plan for the New Abnormal – in the COVID-19
Coronavirus Pandemic
Gleb Tsipursky

Aging with Vision, Hope and Courage in a Time of Crisis
John C. Robinson

Connecting with Nature in a Time of Crisis
Melanie Choukas-Bradley

Going Within in a Time of Crisis
P. T. Mistlberger

Grow Stronger in a Time of Crisis
Linda Ferguson

Handling Anxiety in a Time of Crisis
George Hoffman

Navigating Loss in a Time of Crisis
Jules De Vitto

The Life-Saving Skill of Story
Michelle Auerbach

Virtual Teams – Holding the Center When You Can't Meet
Face-to-Face
Carlos Valdes-Dapena

Virtually Speaking – Communicating at a Distance
Tim Ward and Teresa Erickson

Current Bestsellers from Changemakers Books

Pro Truth
A Practical Plan for Putting Truth Back into Politics
Gleb Tsipursky and Tim Ward
How can we turn back the tide of post-truth politics, fake news, and misinformation that is damaging our democracy? In the lead-up to the 2020 US Presidential Election, *Pro Truth* provides the answers.

An Antidote to Violence
Evaluating the Evidence
Barry Spivack and Patricia Anne Saunders
It's widely accepted that Transcendental Meditation can create peace for the individual, but can it create peace in society as a whole? And if it can, what could possibly be the mechanism?

Finding Solace at Theodore Roosevelt Island
Melanie Choukas-Bradley
A woman seeks solace on an urban island paradise in Washington D.C. through 2016–17, and the shock of the Trump election.

the bottom
a theopoetic of the streets
Charles Lattimore Howard
An exploration of homelessness fusing theology, jazz-verse and intimate storytelling into a challenging, raw and beautiful tale.

The Soul of Activism
A Spirituality for Social Change
Shmuly Yanklowitz
A unique examination of the power of interfaith spirituality to
fuel the fires of progressive activism.

Future Consciousness
The Path to Purposeful Evolution
Thomas Lombardo
An empowering evolutionary vision of wisdom and the human
mind to guide us in creating a positive future.

Preparing for a World that Doesn't Exist – Yet
Rick Smyre and Neil Richardson
This book is about an emerging Second Enlightenment and the
capacities you will need to achieve success in this new, fast-
evolving world.